A Turbo Prolog® Primer

Jean B. Rogers

Stanford University

ADDISON-WESLEY PUBLISHING COMPANY

Reading, Massachusetts ■ Menlo Park, California ■ New York
Don Mills, Ontario ■ Wokingham, England ■ Amsterdam
Bonn ■ Sydney ■ Singapore ■ Tokyo ■ Madrid ■ Bogota
Santiago ■ San Juan

Library of Congress Cataloging-in-Publication Data
Rogers, Jean B.
    A turbo prolog primer.
    Includes index.
    1. Prolog (Computer program language) 2. Turbo
Prolog (Computer program) I. Title.
QA76.73.P76R65 1987   005.13′3   86-28707
ISBN 0-201-12198-0

BCDEFGHIJ-DO-8987

*Dedicated to my family
and especially to Jim*

Preface

PURPOSE

The purpose of *A Turbo Prolog Primer* is to teach the fundamental skills and concepts needed for Prolog programming using the Turbo version of Prolog and the Turbo Prolog software system produced by Borland International. Prolog is a computer programming language that has recently come to the forefront in computer science because of its potential for use in artificial intelligence programming, in information management systems, and in education. Prolog was created in 1972 by the Groupe d'Intelligence Artificielle at the Université d'Aix Marseilles. The name, Prolog, is derived from "programming in logic"; the model upon which Prolog is built is that of formal logic. In the years since its development, the Prolog language has been expanded and improved and has gained favor for a number of computer applications. Reflecting this increasing interest, Borland International has released a low-cost commercial version for use on personal computers.

A Prolog program is a way of representing knowledge. By using Prolog, not only can we represent facts, but we can also represent implications of fact, conclusions based on the facts and implications, and strategies for discovering conclusions. Prolog can be used for creating knowledge-based systems known as expert systems, in which a computer emulates the expertise of a human. Expert systems not only report conclusions but may also hold a dialog with the person who is using the system, asking questions and explaining how it reached its conclusions. Prolog can also be used in natural language processing. Natural language processing involves taking human communication and analyzing it to deduce the knowledge it represents.

Prolog is also gaining popularity for use in education. Some schools use Prolog as an instructional tool and others teach Prolog programming. Since Prolog is easy to learn, even students in elementary school can enjoy using it. Learning Prolog provides experience using a computer as well as experience looking carefully at knowledge about a subject and learning to express it in a formal system.

v

One characteristic of Prolog makes it appropriate for education as well as for artificial intelligence programming. Prolog is good for dynamic, free exploration. The interactive, responsive nature of the Prolog system encourages experimentation and discovery. This flexibility allows the programmer to develop the problem analysis while the program evolves.

The Borland Turbo Prolog system particularly facilitates programming for applications. Software design methods and user-oriented programming are more easily used in Turbo Prolog than in many other Prolog systems.

APPROACH

The instruction in *A Turbo Prolog Primer* is oriented not only toward teaching the Prolog language but more importantly toward helping the reader understand how to think about the programming process for Prolog. Prolog is a declarative language, quite different from most of the currently popular languages. A Prolog program is a set of statements, declaring what is known to be true about the problem to be solved. The programming activity requires writing those statements in a form Prolog can use, specifying facts and rules that are true about the problem and its solution. Prolog then determines the feasibility of the solution based on the knowledge that has been specified.

This book has a practical rather than a theoretical orientation. Prolog has a theoretical basis in logic but the language can be learned and used as a pragmatic tool. Whenever possible, the examples in the book have been chosen to represent effective solutions to typical problems. Appendix B lists references for further reading, many of which provide a more formal, theoretical discussion of Prolog.

Currently, there are a number of versions of Prolog available. They differ not in terms of the concepts they use but only in the way the programs are written down. Throughout the main part of this book, one version of Prolog is used consistently in the examples and the explanations. That version is Turbo Prolog, an integrated system for creating and using Prolog programs. Appendix C contains the form for four other common versions, Edinburgh, C-Prolog, micro-PROLOG and SIMPLE. In the appendix, the parallel forms are given on a chapter by chapter basis, matching the examples in the book. Thus, a person who has available a different version of Prolog can use the information in Appendix C to modify examples from the book to run on the available system.

AUDIENCE

The audience for whom this book was written includes mature learners who are neither experienced in computer programming nor particularly sophisticated in mathematics. The examples throughout the first eight chapters are non-mathematical and generally related to "real world" rather than computer science problems. No computing background is assumed for this audience, so the book attempts to provide the required beginning-level system context. For more advanced details of the Turbo Prolog system, however, readers should use the Turbo Prolog Manual.

This book is also an effective introduction to Prolog for people already quite familiar with computer programming. The appendixes, indexes and examples will facilitate the transfer of knowledge from earlier programming experience to Prolog. The experienced programmer is warned, however, that some new thinking is required for Prolog. The introduction to Part II has been specifically provided o help people adapt their experience in programming procedural languages like Pascal and BASIC to programming in Prolog.

There are several instructional environments where *A Turbo Prolog Primer* would be appropriate as a textbook. Primary among them are courses in computing for students who are not computer science majors. For example, library science, mathematics, business and science courses that teach programming would be well served to teach Prolog.

Another instructional environment where Turbo Prolog could be used is computer science classes where students have experience in procedural programming but need to be introduced to other programming models. For example, many current Survey of Programming Languages courses include Prolog.

A third learning environment is less formal: individuals who want an introduction to Turbo Prolog for their personal interest can use this book. Because answers to the exercises at the end of each section are included in the book, the independent learner has feedback available.

ORGANIZATION

A Turbo Prolog Primer is divided into two parts. The first, Tutorial, introduces all the ideas and notation for the core of the language and system. The second part, Advanced Topics, includes chapters about specific topics and discusses development of larger programs. Part I has extensive narrative explanation of fundamental Prolog concepts. It includes a chapter on making the transition from natural language to programming languages, three chapters on the components from which a Turbo Prolog program is written, and one chapter discussing the processing mechanism that underlies the use of a Prolog program.

Part II begins with an introduction that compares Turbo Prolog with other programming languages and points out the differences for the programmer who is moving from more common languages to Turbo Prolog. The next five chapters, the remainder of Part II, address specific topics: process control, input and output, built-in predicates, arithmetic and program development. The discussions in these chapters are concise and concentrate on specific detail.

PEDAGOGY

The pedagogic technique used is a spiral approach. Concepts are introduced and discussed briefly, then later discussed in greater depth. A number of analogies have been used to facilitate an intuitive understanding of the ideas that underlie the Prolog language.

This book is different from most programming texts, even in Prolog, in that number manipulation is left until late in the presentation. As a result, examples throughout the book are word-oriented rather than mathematical.

At the ends of Chapters 2–5 there are special sections called "Experimenting." In each of these, examples of computer interaction are shown. Readers are urged to use these examples as a basis for exploring the Turbo Prolog enivironment on their own.

At the ends of sections in all ten chapters, exercises are provided. Answers to these exercises are given in Appendix E. In some cases, alternate answers are given, but in all cases readers should bear in mind that there is almost always more than one way to write a computer program for a task and rarely a single way that can be declared "the best program." Each chapter also has review exercises, some of which are suggestions for programs.

The material presented in *A Turbo Prolog Primer* has been used for instruction in courses with computer science and other graduate students, computer science undergraduates and undergraduates from non-computer science majors. Their feedback was a guiding factor in development of the book.

ACKNOWLEDGMENTS

I want to thank again all the people who helped me while I was writing *A Prolog Primer*, from which this book is derived, and all the people who so kindly complimented it, thus encouraging me to keep writing.

Additional thanks to Peter Aiken for the thoughtful review of this manuscript and to the students at the University of Texas, Austin, for their careful reading and comments.

Contents

I

TUTORIAL 1

How to Use This Book 1

II

ADVANCED TOPICS 95

How Turbo Prolog Is Like And Unlike Other Languages 95

10 ■ *Building Larger Programs 159*

Appendixes 177

Index 209

Tutorial

How to Use This Book

A Turbo Prolog Primer can help you learn to program in Prolog whether or not you already know how to program in any computer language.

If you do not already know how to program, you will want to start your reading with Chapter 1 and follow through the whole first part, the Tutorial. When you get to the second part, the Advanced Topics, you may or may not want to read the introduction to that part. The introduction compares Turbo Prolog with other programming languages; the discussion of Turbo Prolog itself begins again in Chapter 6. Understanding the material in Part II does not depend on your learning the content of the introduction, but you may find it interesting.

If you already know how to program in some language other than Prolog, you may want to start your reading in this book with the introduction to Part II. Along with comparing the languages, the introduction points out several specifics where Turbo Prolog programming is different. After you have read the

1

introduction to Part II, you may want to go directly on to the Advanced Topics there, or you may want to read parts of the Tutorial to learn more about particular facets of this language.

Whether you are new to programming or only new to Turbo Prolog, the listing of examples in the book should provide help in writing your own programs.

1

Looking at Language

The purpose of this chapter is to help the learner:

- become aware of patterns in natural language.
- recognize the same semantic content in different syntactic form.
- realize that a specified form of expression can be used to generalize over a number of instances.
- specify which elements will be included in a set
    by one definition.
    by one definition and another.
    by one definition or another.

1.1 NATURAL LANGUAGE AND STRUCTURED FORMS

Language is a way for human beings to communicate ideas. Computer programming languages provide communication between people and computers; natural languages, like English and Chinese, allow people to communicate with other people. Prolog is a programming language. The purpose of this book is to help the reader learn to be a programmer and be able to write Prolog programs using the Turbo Prolog system. Our discussion of the specifics of Prolog, however, does not start until the second chapter of the book. In this first chapter, we will consider typical expressions we use in natural language and look at some ways to simplify those expressions.

We may look forward to the time when we can communicate with computers just as we do with another human, but right now, we are obliged to make some

3

concessions. While Prolog is much more like natural language than are most other programming languages, we still must know how to provide information to Turbo Prolog in a regularized, simplified form. To develop that ability, we will look at some less formal forms and consider how they allow us to organize and generalize the communication we use in natural language.

Natural language is a rich, complex collection of vocabulary, sentence structure and interrelations between sentences. One example of the richness of natural language is that we have many ways of expressing the same idea:

He smashed his toe with the chair.

His injury resulted from dropping a chair on his toe.

His toe was injured by being smashed by a chair.

The chair smashed his toe.

These four sentences all tell of the same event, communicating approximately the same idea. Several key words are the same in each sentence, but their position and focus is different. The meaning of a sentence is called its *semantics*. The physical structure of the sentence is called its *syntax*. In natural language we use many different syntactic forms to communicate the same or only subtly distinct semantics. Using variety in language makes communication more interesting and more precise. In contrast, choosing one pattern and using it repeatedly makes communication simpler and more easily analyzed. In programming, and particularly in Prolog, only a few patterns are used.

General Forms

In the computer programming environment we choose patterns of expression that are simple and then use them repeatedly. Using patterns allows us to skip over some detail and still communicate the idea. We always try to select a form that not only provides a simplified pattern but also allows pieces of information to be grouped together. We can call a form that applies to a number of specific instances a generic form. For example, the smashed toe might be part of a list of injuries being reported.

reported	toe	smashed	chair
reported	finger	cut	glass
reported	knee	skinned	pavement

We can see a general pattern in this list and can use special notation to specify it.

reported <body part> <injury> <instrument>

The angle brackets < > simply indicate the general category rather than the specific items in each specific instance. Specifying this generic form helps organize several events into a group where all share some element of meaning.

When we simplify natural language expressions into these general forms, we lose much of its richness. It is often difficult to draw the fine line between acceptable simplifications and ones that destroy the validity of the statement. For example, we may make reference to something "people do" as a general rule or we may need to know the specific individuals who did a thing. To maintain validity of the information, we must give careful thought and attention to the context and purpose of the grouping.

Alternative Forms

The generic form above might be appropriate for reporting injuries but the smashed toe could well fit into a different pattern. In this case the generic form might be different.

smashed	toe	chair
smashed	crime	FBI
smashed	world-record	runner
smashed	<object>	<instrument>

Choosing the appropriate pattern to group a set of events or facts that belong in a set will depend on the larger context of the elements. By the same token, each individual person will have his or her own view of the larger context. While one person might prefer

smashed <object> <instrument>

another might prefer

smashed <instrument> <object>

or perhaps

<instrument> smashed <object>

None of these choices is inherently better than the others; individual people will have their own favorites. The important point to remember is that it is simplicity and consistency that facilitate communication. This is especially significant in the distilled natural language that is the basis for programming language.

EXERCISES 1.1

1. Write a general form for

ate	soup	lunch
ate	eggs	breakfast
ate	beef	dinner
ate	pie	dinner

2. Write a general form that adds which day's meal it was to the items above.
3. Specify three alternative general forms for the items in Exercise 2.
4. Organize the data from this paragraph into simplified items and then specify a generic form.

This July I have to attend summer school for the first two weeks but the third week I can laze around. The last week in July I have to go to a meeting in New York.

1.2 SEMANTIC NETWORKS

A second way of looking at sentence structure is to use a diagram to represent the activity or relationship in the sentence. There are many kinds of diagrams that are used for this. One way of diagramming sentence information is called a semantic network.

A semantic network consists of words that are objects connected by arrows. Along each arrow a word or phrase is written that indicates the activity or relationship between the objects, as in Figure 1.1.

Semantic networks are particularly useful when a single object appears in more than one sentence. A semantic network can show, for example, that a tornado smashed several buildings, as in Figure 1.2, or that several people eat pizza, as in Figure 1.3.

FIGURE 1.1 Simple Semantic Networks

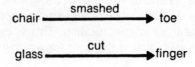

FIGURE 1.2 Network Centering on One Object

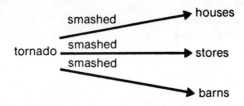

Certain types of relationships carry from one object to another. These relationships are called transitive because the relationship goes across intermediate objects. These, too, are shown well by semantic networks, as in Figure 1.4.

Semantic networks are particularly useful when we want to express a hierarchy of relationships. For example, objects are made up of other objects and are themselves components of other objects. This relationship can be denoted by ISPART, as in Figure 1.5.

Another hierarchical relationship derives from the classification of objects. A relationship that shows classification can be written as ISA, like Figure 1.6.

Sometimes it is clearer to have an event be the central object in a semantic network. An event is an abstract object that acts as the focus of some description. Figure 1.7 shows a semantic network based on a shopping trip.

FIGURE 1.3 Alternative Network Centering on One Object

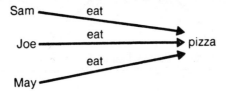

FIGURE 1.4 Semantic Network of Transitive Relationship

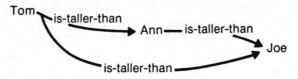

FIGURE 1.5 Semantic Network of ISPART

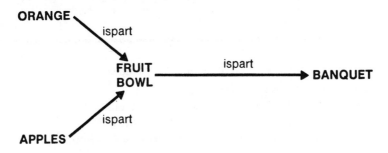

FIGURE 1.6 Semantic Network of ISA

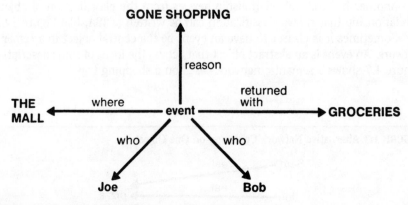

FIGURE 1.7 Semantic Network Centered on an Event

In every case in a semantic network, the arrow and the objects on each end of it express a relationship between the objects. The relationship is directed from one object to the other. We can consider the relationship and the object at the front of the arrow as an attribute and value of the attribute for the object at the base of the arrow. These attribute/value pairs give us a standardized form for representing knowledge about the object and provide a structure for gleaning information from the simplified representation of the knowledge.

EXERCISES 1.2

1. Draw a semantic network for the following examples.

> Joe, Jane and I went to the market.
> I talked Joe into getting watermelon and he talked Jane into it.
> I gave Jane some money so she could pay the bill.
> Joe gave me the car keys but I gave them back to him.

2. Write a natural language interpretation for these three semantic networks.

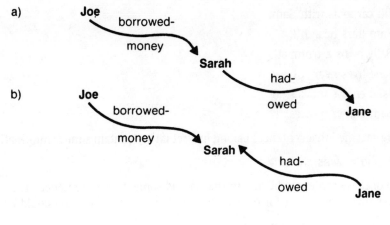

a)

b)

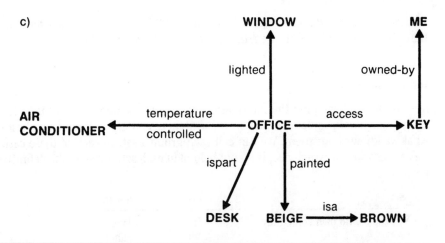

c)

1.3 RECOGNIZING INSTANCES IN SETS

When one has various items, they can be grouped into sets of items. Often the grouping is done according to some general specification. The specification defines which items belong in the grouping and which ones do not. A generic form like those in Section 1.1 is one way of writing the definition for inclusion in the group. For example, assume we have a number of sentences such as the items:

1. Joe owns a bike.
2. Joe enjoys movies.

3. Jill owns three books.
4. Jill carpools with Sam.
5. Sam lives near Jill.
6. Sally owns a trumpet.
7. Jane lives near Jill.
8. Jane enjoys movies.
9. Sam enjoys movies.

Say we specified that sentences belong in a set if they contain similar information.

<who> owns <what>

Some of these sentences belong in the set and some do not. Sentences 1, 3, and 6 above make up the set for ownership. Another definition of a set could be

<who> enjoys movies

In this case only 2, 8 and 9 meet this requirement. We can say that the sentences that meet the requirement are *true* instances of the specifications.

Individuals in Sets

Another way of grouping the information in the nine sentences above is to look at the individual people identified in the sentences and group them according to what we know about them. We can call each group a set. In each of these cases, we can also specify which people do not belong in each set, based on the definition given.

Set	in	not-in
A People who own something	Joe Jill Sally	Jane Sam
B People who enjoy movies	Joe Jane Sam	Jill Sally
C People who carpool with Sam	Jill	Jane Joe Sam Sally
D People who live near Jill	Sam Jane	Joe Sally Jill

To specify who is *not* in one of these sets requires an important assumption: that these nine sentences about five people tell us all there is to know about everybody. Assuming that there is no further information about these people allows us to assume that if we do not know a fact, the fact is not true. This is called the closed world assumption. In this example, we also are avoiding self-references in facts. Thus we are concluding that Sam does not carpool with himself nor does Jill live near herself.

EXERCISES 1.3

1. Using the following sentences, write a generic form that divides the sentences into two groups.

> Sweaters keep you warm.
> Sweaters are good gifts.
> Long sox keep your feet warm.
> Sandals keep you cool.
> Shorts keep you cool, too.
> Flowers make a good gift.

2. Each sentence gives you information about an object. Pick those individual objects out of the sentences above and group them into three groups according to some characteristic stated in the sentences.

3. For each of your three groups above, list all the objects not in each group according to the sentences.

1.4 ONE DEFINITION AND ANOTHER

When we have individuals grouped into sets according to definitions, we can refine that grouping by finding items that meet two specifications. The group consists of items that meet one specification *AND* another specification. For example, in the sentences in Section 1.3, what people own something and enjoy movies? Only Joe meets both of these requirements.

In analyzing the grouping by definition or definitions, a useful tool is a graphic called a Venn diagram. Say we have the following three sets of people and their favorite leisure time activities.

A. Al, Bet, Cat, Den and Ed like reading.

B. Al, Bet, Fred and Gar like movies.

C. Bet, Den, Fred and Hal like plays.

In the Venn diagram in Figure 1.8, each circle encloses the names of people who belong in the specified set. The circles are drawn so that individuals appear in the circle for each grouping they belong to. Each person only appears once, however, so if that person is in two circles, the circles must overlap.

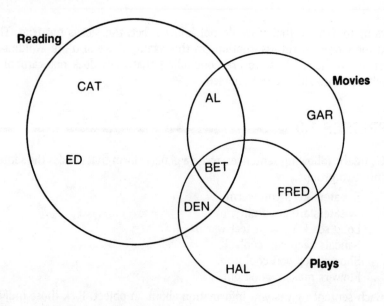

FIGURE 1.8 Venn Diagram of Three Sets

As a result, individuals who meet the specification of liking reading and of liking movies are shown in the overlap of those two circles. People who like all three (movies, reading, and plays) are in the overlap of all three circles. In this example only Bet meets this description. When we specify that each person must meet more than one requirement: that either maintains the grouping size or narrows down the number of people that are part of the grouping. In general, "and" adds restrictions for inclusion in a group, making the group more specific and often smaller.

1.5 ONE DEFINITION OR ANOTHER

In contrast to "and" which narrows down a grouping, "or" expands it. For an item to be part of a group defined by one requirement *OR* another, it only has to meet at least one, instead of both of the specifications. From the original Venn diagram, we can see "reading or movies" contains seven people, the grouping described by "reading or plays" contains everyone but Gar, and "movies or plays" includes everyone but Cat and Ed. Using "or" allows inclusion of items in a set on a more general but still defined basis. In general, "or" removes restrictions for inclusion in a group, making the group less specific and often bigger.

EXERCISES 1.4, 1.5

1. Draw a Venn diagram for these three sets.

   A. People who wear boots: Mike, Sam, Jo and Lou.
   B. People who ride bikes: Jo, Glen and Lou.
   C. People who jog: Ann, Char, Jo and Sam.

2. Identify the set A AND B. Who is in it?

3. Identity the set A AND B AND C. Who is in it?

4. Identify the set A OR B. Who is in it?

5. Who is in the set A OR B OR C?

SUMMARY

Any language has semantics, which is the meaning or the ideas being expressed, and syntax, which is the organizational structure of the language. Natural language is rich and complex, both in its semantics and its syntax. For computer programming, we want to simplify and regularize the syntax without losing too much of the semantics. To adapt natural language to programming, we use generalizations and patterns that simplify our expression of knowledge.

In this chapter we have seen several ways of representing knowledge in an organized and structured manner. Each of the ways makes use of some form or structure to carry information about the knowledge:

- generic forms show patterns
- semantic networks show relationships
- sets and Venn diagrams show groupings.

Items of various kinds can be grouped according to specifications that define which instances are true and which are not true for the specification. The specifications can be joined by "and" which further narrows the grouping, or by "or" which broadens the grouping.

To program in Turbo Prolog, we will use precise forms of expression to convey information to the computer. The purpose of a program is to provide specifications that represent the knowledge we want to use. The precise forms, Turbo Prolog syntax, will be the communication medium. •

EXERCISES CHAPTER 1

1. Identify the concept or concepts described by each phrase below.

   a) The part of a language that conveys meaning and ideas.
   b) The manner by which parts of a language are put together.

    c) The kind of language that (1) Prolog is; (2) English is.

    d) In sets, that which Venn diagrams represent graphically.

    e) A graphic method in which arrows and objects show attribute/value pairs.

    f) Assuming that a set of sentences includes all there is to know about some objects.

    g) A method to help us see patterns and groupings.

    h) In set specification, connectors that widen and narrow the specifications.

2. Draw a semantic network, a Venn diagram, and some generic forms based on this paragraph.

    Pavan had a party. John brought limeade and ice. Sally brought cheese and crackers, but Joe brought cheese too. Jan brought the same kind of cookies that she took to Mike's party last week.

3. Choose an event and describe it in several ways including some of the forms we discussed in this chapter. Compare the descriptions and choose the one you feel best communicates the information.

2

Turbo Prolog: To Define a World

The purpose of this chapter is to help the learner:

■ perceive a Turbo Prolog program as a self-contained world description.
■ state Turbo Prolog facts.
■ recognize the roles of constants and variables.
■ use goals to ask questions for
  confirmation of facts.
  reporting of variable values.

2.1 PROGRAMMING LANGUAGES

A computer is a tool that can solve many different kinds of problems. For a computer to solve a particular problem, it must be given information about that problem. Programming languages are a way for people to communicate with a computer about the particular problem that is to be solved. The programming language is used to provide information about the problem and about the requirements for finding the solution to the problem. There are many different programming languages, but their role is always to communicate specifics of a problem to a computer.

Problems generally fall into one of a number of categories. For example, a problem like space navigation involves a lot of numeric calculations. Other problems, like printing transcripts for students, require taking a quantity of known information and arranging it in a form that people can easily understand. Because of the way programming languages have been designed, different ones match with certain types of problems. That is, the languages have the vocabulary and means of expression to communicate requirements that are typical of certain kinds of problems.

Turbo Prolog

Prolog is a programming language designed for a particular kind of problem. It is a convenient way to describe a self-contained world of knowledge. Tasks that can be carried out by following precise specifications can be done in a Turbo Prolog world that knows those specifications. For example, translation from one computer language to another can be done by a Turbo Prolog world that knows the translation rules. Another role for Turbo Prolog worlds is as an information resource. The world will provide selected information at the request of a person. This is the Turbo Prolog role we will focus on during the first part of this book.

The description of the world will consist of facts and rules. Once we have the world description, we can ask questions about that world by specifying them in the form of goals. The questions we ask and the answers we receive make using Turbo Prolog like holding a conversation with the computer, a conversation about the world described in the program.

The questions we ask will not be limited to requests for simple facts; Turbo Prolog will use the rules to combine facts about the world to find answers to complex questions. The questions themselves, as specified in the goals, are descriptive. They describe requirements of the desired answer rather than specifying how to find the answer. The facts and rules describe the world in the Turbo Prolog program; the questions describe the kinds of answers to be provided from the world. Because of its character, Prolog is called a descriptive language. Neither the world nor the goals will give Turbo Prolog instructions about what actions should be carried out to find the answer. That process is embedded in the Turbo Prolog system.

Of course, the answers will be constrained by the limits of the data it has been given in the description of the world. A Turbo Prolog program knows only about the world of knowledge that has been specified. Similarly, the description of this world need not match the world of our normal experience. If we choose to define a world in which "up" is the same as "down," Turbo Prolog will not object. Turbo Prolog allows a programmer to define a knowledge base and then explore that knowledge with questions.

A Base of Facts

A fundamental part of a Turbo Prolog description of a world is the facts it contains. Each fact is like a sentence, declaring a piece of information about one or more objects in the world. For example,

```
capital(texas,austin).
```

This fact shows that there is a relation between two objects, texas and austin.

In providing Turbo Prolog with a set of facts, we will follow rules as to how we write them. These rules, which are called *syntax* rules, are quite simple but very important. The name that defines the relationship appears first, then the names of the objects appear within parentheses, separated by a comma. Like a sentence, the fact ends with a period (.).

Syntax Rules: Facts
- relationship name first
- objects in parentheses, comma between
- period (full stop) at end

The relationship name and the object names start with lower-case letters. This is to indicate to Turbo Prolog that these are names of specific objects and that the names will not change; they are called constants. Notice that there are no spaces within the fact. If we want to use a name that includes a space, we use an underscore in place of the space,

```
capital(new_mexico,santa_fe).
```

These two examples use the same relationship name, capital. We can interpret these facts as meaning "The capital of Texas is Austin" and "The capital of New Mexico is Santa Fe." The order of the object names and the interpretation of the facts are freely chosen by the programmer who designs the facts.

Turbo Prolog requires that an attribute or relationship and its objects, known also as the *predicate* and its *arguments*, maintain the same pattern throughout a program. Most commonly, predicates we use will have two or three arguments, but occasionally we will need more. The number of arguments for a predicate is known as its *arity*.

In a Turbo Prolog program, we will specify the facts in our world using two sections

- predicates — the form of the predicates and their objects
- clauses — the individual facts

The predicates section, which appears first, specifies the generic form of facts using the relationship name and a specification for each of the objects that will appear in the fact. The objects will be specified by their type so that Turbo Prolog will recognize what kind of object will appear in the fact. Later we will use other types of objects such as numbers, but for now all our objects are names, known in Turbo Prolog as symbols.

The predicates section begins with a keyword that identifies the section.

```
predicates
    capital(symbol,symbol)
```

The facts appear in the clauses section.

```
clauses
    capital(california,sacramento).
    capital(nevada,carson_city).
```

Compare the use of periods in these two sections. Notice that each fact is terminated by a period in the clauses section but predicate statements need not be. Clause is the formal Turbo Prolog term for a sentence that describes part of the world in a Turbo Prolog program.

A collection of Turbo Prolog facts in a program is called a *base* or a *database*. We could imagine a set of facts like these examples that specifies the capital of all states in the United States. Each state and capital city pair would appear separately in an individual fact. Figure 2.1 shows a Turbo Prolog base with a few states and capitals.

In the same base of facts, we can include other facts about some of the same objects

```
weather(texas,summer,hot).
```

or other completely independent objects

```
color(sox,green).
```

Sometimes only one object name appears within the parentheses of the fact. In such a predicate, with an arity of one, the name in front of the parentheses usually represents an attribute or characteristic of the object. For example,

```
female(mary).
```

Each fact must have the type of its objects and its form specified in the predicates section before the facts can appear in the clauses section. Within the clauses section, all facts of the same form must be grouped together but the groups need not appear in the order that the forms appear in the predicates section.

FIGURE 2.1 Facts — States and Capitals

```
predicates
    capital(symbol,symbol)
clauses
    capital(washington,olympia).
    capital(oregon,salem).
    capital(california,sacramento).
    capital(arizona,phoenix).
    capital(new_mexico,santa_fe).
    capital(texas,austin).
    capital(nevada,carson_city).
```

In creating a base of facts, the programmer has responsibility for choosing the pattern and putting the names of objects in the appropriate position in a predicate. The pattern will be based on the meaning of the facts to the programmer. The meaning of the program is called the *semantics* of the program. Semantics stands in contrast to syntax, which, as we said earlier, is the way the program is written down. The computer's processing is based on syntax, not semantics.

EXERCISES 2.1

1. Write a Turbo Prolog database of predicates and clauses for facts based on these sentences.
   The book is on the table.
   The book is on the third shelf.
   John owns a dog.
   Jim owns a cat.

2. What might these facts mean? Give at least two interpretations.

   ```
   mother(sarah,jane).
   father(joe,sam).
   ```

3. An old joke: Which is better, a ham sandwich or eternal happiness? Well, nothing is better than eternal happiness, and a ham sandwich is better than nothing. Therefore, a ham sandwich is better than eternal happiness. What does this have to do with Turbo Prolog facts?

2.2 QUERIES USING GOALS

When we have a base of facts, we can use Turbo Prolog to ask questions about the world we have described in the database by giving Turbo Prolog a goal. Goals follow the same syntax rules that facts follow. The Turbo Prolog system supplies the prompt "Goal:". For example,

```
Goal: capital(oregon,salem).
```

This kind of question is a direct request for confirmation that a fact is in the base that has been given. Assume we have a base that consists of a set of facts, one giving the capital city for a selected set of states in the United States (see Figure 2.1) specified by predicates and clauses. If we give the program the goal

```
Goal: capital(oregon,salem).
```

Turbo Prolog would respond

```
True
```

If we entered

    Goal: capital(oregon,portland).

Turbo Prolog would respond

    False

If we entered

    Goal: capital(ontario,toronto).

Turbo Prolog would answer

    False

not because Toronto is not the capital of Ontario, but because that fact is not in the information we provided in our description. We describe a world in our database. Turbo Prolog can only respond from the data in the base, answering "false" if a fact is not in that world.

Turbo Prolog checks to see if a fact exists in a database by using pattern matching, comparing to see whether the specific items in the goal match those in a fact. When given a goal, Turbo Prolog compares the first fact in the database with the expression given in the goal. If it does not match, Turbo Prolog moves on to the next fact to try the match, and continues the process until one of two things happens. Either it succeeds in making the match, whereupon it reports "true," or it checks the base clear through to the end and fails to find the match, so it reports "false." Turbo Prolog responds "false" to both these goals

    Goal: capital(oregon,portland).
    Goal: capital(ontario,toronto).

because it does not find matching facts in the base. Similarly, small typographic errors create completely different words. Thus,

    Goal: capital(texas,asutin).

would be answered

    False

Because Turbo Prolog is matching the pattern of the fact with the pattern in the question, details such as the spelling and the order of the object names must be attended to carefully.

Variables

We will sometimes want Turbo Prolog to check a piece of information against a database and report a "true" or "false" to us. More frequently, however, we will want Turbo Prolog to fill in the name of an object that belongs in a relationship. To do this, we will again provide a goal that contains the pattern we are looking for, but in the place of the name we want, we put a variable name. It is called a *variable* because it can stand in place of various objects. The concept of a variable stands in contrast to that of a *constant*. A constant name always refers to the same object. In Turbo Prolog, we specify that a name is a variable by beginning the name with an upper-case letter. For example, in

```
Goal: capital(nevada,City).
```

City is a variable because it starts with an upper-case letter, C. If we asked this question of our base in Figure 2.1, the response would be

```
City = carson_city
1 solution
```

We could as well have used any set of letters to represent the variable as long as the first is upper-case. Thus the question

```
Goal: capital(washington,XYZ).
```

will get the response

```
XYZ = olympia
1 solution
```

Since XYZ is a variable, we can use it again

```
Goal: capital(california,XYZ).
```

to be told

```
XYZ = sacramento
1 solution
```

Different people choose different kinds of words for variable names. Some people prefer a letter like X which is short and fast to use. Others prefer words like City, which may convey more meaning. Meaningful names help programmers make fewer mistakes.

We can use variables for any of the objects within the parentheses. For

```
Goal: capital(State,phoenix).
```

we will get the response

```
State = arizona
1 solution
```

and for

```
Goal: capital(State,santa_fe).
State = new_mexico
1 solution
```

but for

```
Goal: capital(ontario,City).
```

we will be told "no solution" since the expression in the goal has no match in our database, no matter what object the variable stands for. We are not limited to one variable in each goal. We might ask

```
Goal: capital(State,City).
```

Turbo Prolog's response to this kind of goal is discussed in the next section.

While variables can stand in place of any of the objects named in a fact, they cannot be used in place of the relationship name. Arguments may be variables, but predicates may not. Turbo Prolog will indicate an error has been made:

```
Goal: Connection(oregon,salem).
404 Undeclared predicate or misspelling
```

EXERCISES 2.2

1. Write a Turbo Prolog base to match these statements, then give examples of goals with variables that could be used with the facts.
   The book is on the table.
   The book is on the third shelf.
   John owns a dog.
   Jim owns a cat.

2. Given these facts in a base

   ```
   owns(john,dog,midget)
   owns(john,cow,jersey)
   ```

   what will be the response to

   ```
   Goal: owns(Thief,cow,jersey).
   Goal: owns(john,A,midget).
   Goal: owns(john,cow,Breed).
   ```

3. Specify advantages and disadvantages for each of the variable names in Exercise 2.

2.3 MULTIPLE SOLUTIONS

In the last section, when Turbo Prolog returned the name of an object in response to a goal, it also reported "1 solution". In each of those examples, there was only one fact in the database that matched the specifications of the goal. Frequently there will be more than one fact that matches.

Consider a base that consists of facts about a product and the raw material from which it is made. Figure 2.2 shows such a base. If we enter the goal

```
Goal: made_into(plums,What).
```

Turbo Prolog responds

```
What = prunes
What = wine
2 solutions
```

There are two matches in our database that provide Turbo Prolog a solution to this goal. In a similar manner,

```
Goal: made_into(What,wine).
```

gets the responses

```
What = grapes
What = apples
What = plums
3 solutions
```

We have already mentioned that questions can contain more than one variable. Consider the goal

```
Goal: made_into(Source,Product).
```

Because we have variables in the places of both arguments in this predicate, the goal will be able to match with any and all of the facts in our base.

```
Goal: made_into(Source,Product).
Source = plums,    Product = prunes
Source = grapes,   Product = raisins
Source = apples,   Product = sauce
Source = grapes,   Product = wine
Source = apples,   Product = wine
Source = plums,    Product = wine
6 solutions
```

FIGURE 2.2 Raw Materials and Products

```
predicates
    made_into(symbol,symbol)
clauses
    made_into(plums,prunes).
    made_into(grapes,raisins).
    made_into(apples,sauce).
    made_into(grapes,wine).
    made_into(apples,wine).
    made_into(plums,wine).
```

Turbo Prolog has worked through the database and reported constant values for every fact that could be matched to the goal. They are reported in the order in which they were found in the base.

EXERCISES 2.3

Suppose you have the database

```
predicates
    do(symbol,symbol)
clauses
    do(monday,call_agent).
    do(friday,get_tickets).
    do(tuesday,get_money).
    do(monday,write_home).
    do(friday,pack).
    do(thursday,study).
    do(tuesday,study).
```

1. What will be Turbo Prolog's responses to the following questions?

```
Goal: do(monday,What).
Goal: do(tuesday,What).
Goal: do(When,study).
```

2. How many responses will be given to

```
Goal: do(When,What).
```

2.4 CONJUNCTIONS ("AND")

More complex queries can be made in Turbo Prolog by writing goals using a conjunction. The conjunction can be written two ways: the word "and" or the comma ",," which is read as "and". For example, the goals

```
Goal: made_into(It,raisins), made_into(It,wine).
Goal: made_into(It,raisins) and made_into(It,wine).
```

ask "What thing is there that raisins are made of and wine is also made of?" In the first part of this book we will use "and" but later we will use the shorter ",," form. A variable name within the goal (between the : and the .) can only represent one object name at a time. That is, when a variable appears more than once in a question, the only matches that can be made will have the same constant name in every place where that variable name appears. Thus Turbo Prolog will answer

```
Goal: made_into(What,raisins) and
            made_into(What,wine).
What = grapes
1 solution
```

There is only one successful match to the complete goal. Even though part (the second part) has some matches in the database, no others match both parts. If, however, the goal is

```
Goal: made_into(What,raisins) and
            made_into(Else,wine).
```

Turbo Prolog responds

```
 What = grapes,  Else = grapes
·What = grapes,  Else = apples
 What = grapes,  Else = plums
 3 solutions
```

Turbo Prolog has made multiple matches and reported the constants for each variable each time. This is possible because What and Else are two separate variables in this question. They may be matched to the same constant, but do not have to be.

More interesting is a database with several different predicates. If we add some facts about colors to our world we can ask "What red things can be made into wine?" To add facts about colors to our database we must also add to the predicates section, to specify the generic form of our new predicate. Our expanded predicates section is

```
predicates
   color(symbol,symbol)
   made_into(symbol,symbol)
```

Now we can enter the individual facts about color in the clauses section. Again, all the facts with the same predicate form are grouped together. See Figure 2.3 for the complete base.

Now we can ask

```
Goal: made_into(Thing,wine) and
            color(red,Thing).
```

and be told

```
Thing = grapes
Thing = apples
2 solutions
```

or

```
Goal: made_into(Thing,Product) and
            color(red,Product).
```

```
Thing = grapes,  Product = wine
Thing = apples,  Product = wine
Thing = plums,   Product = wine
3 solutions
```

Advanced Variable Uses

There are two uses of variables that do not follow the straightforward idea of the variable that we have discussed so far. These are uses that, while not important to the Turbo Prolog we have seen up to this point, will be very useful for more sophisticated programs.

Turbo Prolog has a special variable name, the underscore "_", which can be read "don't care." It is used mainly as a place holder and can match any constant, any time. Given the goal

```
Goal: made_into(_,prunes).
```

Turbo Prolog will respond

```
True
```

that prunes are made of something, according to the knowledge contained in the database. The variable _ is not associated with a specific name, so it is anonymous. A constant is the name of a specific object. A variable can represent a number of constants, but only represents one at any one time. In a goal, the variable represents a specific object and the constant name of that object is reported to the user. The anonymous variable indicates that there is some

---

FIGURE 2.3 Raw Materials, Products and Colors

```
predicates
   color(symbol,symbol)
   made_into(symbol,symbol)
clauses
   made_into(plums,prunes).
   made_into(grapes,raisins).
   made_into(apples,sauce).
   made_into(grapes,wine).
   made_into(apples,wine).
   made_into(plums,wine).
   color(red,grapes).
   color(white,grapes).
   color(purple,plums).
   color(red,apples).
   color(red,wine).
   color(white,wine).
```

constant in the fact in the specified position, but that the questioner is not concerned about what object it is. If a goal has two anonymous variables, the constants in those places need not be the same as they would be with a non-anonymous variable.

The second variation on use of variables is to use them in facts in the database. When a fact is part of a complex definition, it sometimes needs an object, but not necessarily a specific object, as part of the fact. For example,

```
hidden_in(the_dark,Any_object).
```

is a legal fact according to Turbo Prolog syntax rules. Do not be concerned if you cannot see a sensible use for this now; later you will.

EXERCISES 2.4

Suppose you have the database

```
predicates
    do(symbol,symbol)
clauses
    do(monday,call_agent).
    do(friday,get_tickets).
    do(tuesday,get_money).
    do(monday,write_home).
    do(friday,pack).
    do(thursday,study).
    do(tuesday,study).
```

1. I want to know what else I have to do on the same day I pack.

    ```
    Goal: do(Day,pack) and do(Day,Task).
    ```

    What will Turbo Prolog say?

2. How can I just ask if I set aside study time, never mind when?

3. How can I find out if I have other things to do on my study days?

SUMMARY

Turbo Prolog is a descriptive language, designed to define a knowledge base (also called a database) and ask questions of that base. Turbo Prolog facts are part of the base. Turbo Prolog facts are made up of attribute/relationship names followed by object names (arguments). The programmer has responsibility for selecting the form of the facts and understanding the associated meaning. The names of objects in facts are typically constant names, although they can be variables. The attribute/relationship (predicate) names must be constants. A Turbo Prolog program includes predicates and clauses sections.

Two types of questions can be asked of a Turbo Prolog database. Turbo Prolog will answer "true" or "false" to questions for confirmation of a fact. If Turbo Prolog is asked questions with variables, it will return constant names that will create a match between patterns in the question and patterns in the base. A Turbo Prolog query can be used both to check for a true instance in the base or to find a constant that specifies a true instance. If there are multiple constants that specify these instances, Turbo Prolog will report them all.

Goals can contain a conjunction, with a comma or the word "and" used to join the parts. A variable name stands for one constant at any one time, even if it appears in more than one place in a conjunction. •

SYNTAX SUMMARY

Facts

```
predicate(<object1>,<object2>,...).
```

Goals

```
Goal: predicate(<object1>,<object2>,...).
Goal: predicate1(<object1.1>,<object1.2>...),
            predicate2(<object2.2>,...),...
```

Program

```
predicates
    <predicatename(<word>,<word>,...)>
    <predicatename(<word>,<word>,...)>
clauses
    <fact>
    <fact>
    <fact>
```

constants begin with lower-case letters

variables begin with upper-case letters
    _ anonymous variable

, and

EXPERIMENTING WITH CHAPTER 2

Purpose:
    To see: interactive, conversational nature
            creating a program
            running the program
            asking questions

Computers, being general purpose tools, are able to do many things. For a computer to do Turbo Prolog, it must have a large set of instructions to tell it how. These instructions (called software) are stored somewhere, either on a disk that you put in the computer or in a permanent storage area in the computer system.

When you are ready to use Turbo Prolog on a computer, you (the user) must indicate that intention to the computer, so the system will make the Turbo Prolog software available. Assuming you are using an IBM-PC with the current directory set to the disk with Turbo Prolog, you type in

```
> prolog
```

and the computer responds by displaying a screen with system information. Pressing the space bar moves to the next screen, the main programming environment of Turbo Prolog. There are many different things you can direct the system to do in this environment. You will want to learn about them eventually, but to begin you only need to use a few of them.

Two main processes are involved in using Turbo Prolog. The first is creating the program, done using the editor. The second is running the program, when answers are produced in response to goals.

To begin, key in an "e" to activate the editor. A blinking underscore, called the cursor, will appear in the large box on the left. These boxes are called windows. As you type in your program, it appears in the edit window at the cursor. If you need to make corrections, use the four direction arrows (on the number pad on the right part of the keyboard) to move the cursor to just past the mistake. Then use the backspace key to delete the wrong characters, then type in the correct ones.

When you are satisfied with the program, key in "ESC" to exit the editor, then "r" to run the program. Turbo Prolog will begin to process your program. If there are errors that Turbo Prolog can recognize in the program, it will put you back into the editor with the cursor where the problem is. When there are no errors, the word

```
Goal:
```

and the cursor will appear in the dialog window. Now as you type in goals, Turbo Prolog will give you answers to your questions. If Turbo Prolog cannot understand the goal you type (usually because of a typo), it will give you an error message and put the cursor back at the goal. You can correct errors here using the same methods you use in the editor. Figure 2.4 shows an example of the display of an interaction as it appears on an IBM-PC.

If you want to repeat a goal, use the F8 key to retrieve the most recent one. You may also want to retrieve the last goal and make changes in it with the cursor to ask a slightly different question.

When you are finished giving the program goals, press the "ESC" key to stop the program run. A "q" will close down the Turbo Prolog system. Before it stops, the system will ask if you want to save the program. If you save it, you

FIGURE 2.4 An Example of a Display

```
  Run    Compile    Edit    Options    Files    Setup    Quit

┌────────────────── Editor ──────────────┐  ┌─────── Dialog ────────────┐
 Text: 275  Free:65100  Indent Insert NEWS    Goal : capital(oregon,salem).
 predicates                                   True
   capital(symbol,symbol)                     Goal : capital(arizona,lobo).
 clauses                                      False
   capital(washington,olympia).               Goal : capital(arizona,What).
   capital(oregon,salem).                     What=phoenix
   capital(california,sacramento).            1 Solution
   capital(arizona,phoenix).                  Goal : capital(What,olympia).
   capital(new_mexico,santa_fe).              What=washington
   capital(texas,austin).                     1 Solution
   capital(nevada,carson_city).               Goal : capital(ontario,X).
                                              No Solution
                                              Goal :
                                           └───────────────────────────┘

┌────────────────── Message ──────────────┐  ┌─────── Trace ─────────────┐
 Compiling NEWSTATE.PRO
 capital
 capital
 capital

F8:Previous line  F9:Edit  S-F9:View windows  S-F10:Resize window  Esc:Stop exec
```

can use it again without retyping it. If you respond "y" to the question about saving the text, Turbo Prolog will save it under the name WORK.PRO on your disk. Alternatively, you can first use the filer "f" to save the program. Turbo Prolog will ask you for a name and will record the program as a file under that name on your disk. Use the filer the next time to load the file from the disk. Then you can modify it with the editor or run it as before.

You may want to key in and save the example programs from this chapter and those following. Throughout this book, many examples are reused and expanded upon. Keeping a set of files will make future experimenting easier.

EXERCISES CHAPTER 2 ▬▬▬▬▬▬▬▬▬

1. Identify the Turbo Prolog concept or concepts described by each phrase below.
   a) The part of a fact that shows the relationship.
   b) The mechanism for joining more than one fact in a query.
   c) The component that can be matched to constants or variables.
   d) How a world is described in Turbo Prolog.
   e) The variable that can be read as "don't care."
   f) What Turbo Prolog means when it reports a constant for a variable.
   g) How Turbo Prolog responds to a query about a fact with no variables.

2. For each statement, find one answer.
   a) In the following fact, find the predicate.

   ```
   carpet(Room,beige).
   ```

   b) In the following fact, find an argument.

   ```
   carpet(Room,beige).
   ```

   c) In the following fact, find a constant.

   ```
   carpet(Room,beige).
   ```

   d) In the following fact, find a variable.

   ```
   carpet(Room,beige).
   ```

3. Write a Turbo Prolog program for the following.
   a) A set of facts with the name and birthplace of everyone in your family.
   b) A query to see who was born where.
   c) A query to see if two people were born in the same place.
   d) Additional facts for the database about the month people were born.
   e) Pick a month and write a query to see if anyone was born then.
   f) Pick a town and a month and write a query to see who was born there, then.

3

Extending the World Definition: Turbo Prolog Rules

The purpose of this chapter is to help the learner:

■ define and use Turbo Prolog rules, including
> simple rules.
> compound rules.
> multiple rules.
> rules based on rules.

■ understand and use recursive rules.

■ recognize the sources of some problems in using recursion.

3.1 RULES

We use Turbo Prolog by asking questions. Facts form the basis for the answers that we get in response to the questions. Facts are statements that are true in our database, and thus are the fundamental building blocks of the database that describes a world. We can expand the description of the world we have defined by adding *rules* to the database. These rules, which are built on facts, or on other rules and facts, add another dimension to the informational power of Turbo Prolog's responses.

A Turbo Prolog rule has two parts:

1. a conclusion and
2. the requirements for the conclusion.

The rule specifies that the conclusion will be considered true if the requirements component is found to be true. To answer a question based on a rule, the system uses the data available in the base that tells it about the requirements component. If all the requirements can be found to be true, then the conclusion is true.

Syntax of Rules

Turbo Prolog rules can be written in two forms. The general forms for Turbo Prolog rules are

```
<conclusion> :- <requirements>.
<conclusion> if <requirements>.
```

The conclusion, which is called the *head* of the rule, is followed either by the word "if" or by :-. The remainder of the rule specifies one or more requirements. The part after the "if" or the :- is called the *body* of the rule. A fact is actually a rule with no body. In the early part of this book we will use the "if" form.

Syntax Rules: Rules

- conclusion in head (one predicate)
- requirements in body (zero or more predicates)
- "if" or :- between head and body, if any
- period (full stop) at end

As an example of a rule, we might say we can conclude that "the sky is blue today if today's weather outlook is described as fair." In Turbo Prolog, the rule in this example could be expressed as

```
sky(blue) if outlook(fair).
```

Assume we have a database with some facts from today's weather report,

```
outlook(fair).
high(seventies).
low(fifties).
rain(none).
```

To this base we add the rule

```
sky(blue) if outlook(fair).
```

Now if we ask

```
Goal: sky(blue).
```

the system will respond

```
True
```

Since we asked about sky(blue), Turbo Prolog looked for a matching pattern in the database. It found the pattern as the head of a rule, the rule that the sky is blue if the outlook is fair. It then had to establish the truth of the items in the body. In this case, it found the fact that the outlook is fair. Turbo Prolog concluded from this fact, through the rule we have given it, that the sky is blue. Note that, having found the rule and discovered that there is a body containing requirements, it goes back to the beginning of the database to begin searching for the facts to satisfy the requirements.

The structure of a Turbo Prolog rule allows us to specify a conclusion in the head that depends on the requirements indicated in the body. A fact is a rule with no requirement component, so it is a conclusion that is always true.

EXERCISES 3.1

1. Using the above database about weather plus the rule

   ```
   need(umbrella) if rain(heavy).
   ```

   what will Turbo Prolog respond to

   ```
   Goal: need(umbrella).
   ```

2. Write a rule that indicates one may wear shorts if the high is in the seventies.

3. Write a rule that says to plan a picnic if there is no rain.

3.2 RULES WITH VARIABLES

While the previous rule is interesting, it might be more useful to define a rule that made reference to a specific day. With this kind of rule, we could generalize over a number of days' weather. For example,

```
color(sky,blue,Day) if weather(Day,fair).
```

Within this rule, there are constants and a variable. The variable, Day, allows the rule to be applied to more than one instance of fair weather. The constants show the specifics of the rule, that fair weather means a blue sky. The variable stands for one single day throughout the rule. That is, fair weather Monday tells us about Monday's sky color only, not any other day's. In Turbo Prolog, this is indicated by the use of the same variable name in both the conclusion and the requirements of the rule. The variable in the rule can refer to different days at different times, but it will refer to only one day at any one time.

Rules will appear in a database as clauses. As we did with facts, we use the predicates section to specify the generic form for rules. In the predicates section, the head of the rule is listed including the type of the objects that are arguments of the predicate. The rule itself will appear in the clauses section with the facts.

The program still includes two sections. A base about this week's weather would now be

```
predicates
    weather(symbol,symbol)
    color(symbol,symbol,symbol)
clauses
    weather(sunday,fair).
    weather(monday,overcast).
    weather(tuesday,fair).
    weather(wednesday,fair).
    weather(thursday,overcast).
    weather(friday,rainy).
    weather(saturday,overcast).
    color(sky,blue,Day) if weather(Day,fair).
```

Now if we ask

```
Goal: color(sky,blue,Day).
```

Turbo Prolog will respond

```
Day = sunday
Day = tuesday
Day = wednesday
3 solutions
```

We have written our query using Day for the variable. Turbo Prolog will not confuse our use of Day as the variable name in the question with our use of the same word in the rule. The word Day in our query is not the same as the word Day in the rule from Turbo Prolog's point of view. A variable is considered the same for all appearances in one Turbo Prolog clause, up to the period at the end. Facts and rules are both *clauses,* and so in fact are goals. A variable must be associated with the same constant throughout a clause but only within that clause. This is called the *scope* of the variable.

Because of their scope, Day in the rule and Day in the query are different to Turbo Prolog. They happen to appear in the same position in a matching predicate, but it is the position instead of the word that is important. We could use another variable instead. The system has its own internal representation for the variables in rules so that we are free to use any variable we choose in questions. For example, we might choose When.

```
Goal: color(sky,blue,When).
When = sunday
When = tuesday
When = wednesday
3 solutions
```

If we add another rule to our base which says

```
color(sky,grey,Day) if weather(Day,overcast).
```

and ask a more general question

```
Goal: color(sky,Which,When).
```

Turbo Prolog will tell us

```
Which = blue,   When = sunday
Which = blue,   When = tuesday
Which = blue,   When = wednesday
Which = grey,   When = monday
Which = grey,   When = thursday
Which = grey,   When = saturday
6 solutions
```

Notice that the search came to the blue-sky rule first and reported all the days with blue sky before moving on to the grey-sky days. Even though we used Day as the variable in both rules, the two rules are separate and there is no association between them.

One thing Turbo Prolog cannot do is work from conclusions back to requirements. The rule is not symmetric. For example, if we add the fact

```
color(sky,blue,christmas).
```

then ask

```
Goal: weather(christmas,fair).
```

Turbo Prolog will answer

```
False
```

To help understand this directionality, think of the :- as an arrow pointing to the left and the arrow pointing from the requirements to the conclusion. The reason underlying this asymmetry is that Turbo Prolog rules mean

conclusion "if" requirements

not

conclusion "if and only if" requirements

Thus,

```
happy(jean) if day(christmas).
```

means "Jean will be happy if it is Christmas" not "Jean will be happy only if it is Christmas" or "If Jean is happy it must be Christmas."

EXERCISES 3.2

1. If we added a rule to our weather database

       bask(sun,When) if weather(When,fair).
   and ask

       Goal: bask(sun,Day).
   how will Turbo Prolog respond?
2. Write a rule that says to take an umbrella on a rainy day.
3. Write a rule that says to take an umbrella on an overcast day.

3.3 RULES WITH CONJUNCTIONS

Usually, our rules are designed for conclusions contingent on more than one requirement. To specify more than one requirement, we list them in the right hand part of the rule, with the word "and" or with commas (,) between them. The conjunction works just as it did with questions in Chapter 2. Thus, for example,

       happy(birders,Day) if weather(Day,fair) and
                           active(birds,Day).

could be read "Birders are happy on a day if the weather that day is fair and birds are active that day."

In this rule, notice that the second part of the body is shown on the next line. Turbo Prolog clauses can be spread out like this because it is the period that signals the end of the clause, not the end of a line. The clause may be broken up wherever a space is appropriate. Different layouts are chosen partly due to the size of the rules and partly due to programmer preference. Easy readability should be the main goal in choosing layout.

We can add this rule to our database from above but to use it we will also have to add facts to match the second part of the body of the rule (i.e. active(birds,Day).). If we add

       active(birds,sunday).
       active(birds,tuesday).
       active(birds,thursday).

we now have the database in Figure 3.1. Using this base we ask

       Goal: happy(birders,When).

```
predicates
    weather(symbol,symbol)
    color(symbol,symbol,symbol)
    happy(symbol,symbol)
    active(symbol,symbol)
clauses
    weather(sunday,fair).
    weather(monday,overcast).
    weather(tuesday,fair).
    weather(wednesday,fair).
    weather(thursday,overcast).
    weather(friday,rainy).
    weather(saturday,overcast).
    color(sky,blue,Day) if weather(Day,fair).
    color(sky,grey,Day) if weather(Day,overcast).
    happy(birders,Day) if weather(Day,fair) and
                          active(birds,Day).
    active(birds,sunday).
    active(birds,tuesday).
    active(birds,thursday).
```

FIGURE 3.1 Weather and Birding

Turbo Prolog tells us

```
When = sunday
When = tuesday
2 solutions
```

Notice that the system only reports days when both parts of the requirements component can be confirmed with the variable representing the same specific day. According to our rules, even though the birds were active Thursday, Thursday's overcast weather prevented birders from being happy.

When you as a programmer are writing the Turbo Prolog form of a rule you are defining, you may have trouble deciding how many variables to use and where to put them. For many people, it is easier to develop the correct clause if they focus on how they would *confirm* that a constant meets the rule than if they focus their thinking on how to *generate* the constants they want. Instead of thinking about getting information out of the database, think about an individual or an object and list the specifications that must be true in the database about that individual or object. After the rule is written, be sure that the form of the requirements in the body of a rule matches the form of the facts in the database.

EXERCISES 3.3

1. Write a rule that says birders will have mixed feelings about a day when it is rainy and birds are active.
2. According to our base, when will this happen?

3.4 RULES BASED ON OTHER RULES

The requirements in a rule need not only be facts; they can also be conclusions from other rules. For example,

```
skyeyes(Person,Day) if color(sky,Hue,Day) and
                          eyes(Hue,Person).
```

would allow us to ask whose eyes matched the sky some day this week. It would only work if our earlier database (Figure 3.1) were augmented with some facts about the color of some people's eyes. For example,

```
eyes(grey,sue).
```

Three pairs of days and "sue" would be reported in response to

```
Goal: skyeyes(Who,When).
Who = sue   When = monday
Who = sue   When = thursday
Who = sue   When = saturday
3 solutions
```

In this particular example, the variable, Hue, appears only in the requirements component and not in the conclusion component. Nonetheless, Hue is involved in the matching needed to follow this rule. We will return to this example in Chapter 4 when we discuss the way Turbo Prolog follows its pattern-matching path through these rules.

Multiple Rules

In addition to complex rules that use "and" in the requirements component, rules can use "or" (;) to specify more than one possible set of requirements for a single conclusion. For this circumstance, however, there is a better solution. In our database, we can have more than one rule that yields the same conclusion. These multiple rules will have the same predicate in their heads but different bodies. Say we use our database about weather and birders, add facts

```
observed(rarebird,wednesday).
observed(rarebird,friday).
```

and add the rule

```
happy(birders,Day) if observed(rarebird,Day).
```

Our complete database is shown in Figure 3.2.

Now we have two ways to conclude that birders will be happy. If we ask

```
Goal: happy(birders,When).
When = sunday
When = tuesday
When = wednesday
When = friday
4 solutions
```

The first two days were reported by using the first rule; the second two by using the second rule. If we add another fact,

```
observed(rarebird,tuesday).
```

FIGURE 3.2 Extended Weather and Birding

```
predicates
    weather(symbol,symbol)
    color(symbol,symbol,symbol)
    happy(symbol,symbol)
    active(symbol,symbol)
    observed(symbol,symbol)
clauses
    weather(sunday,fair).
    weather(monday,overcast).
    weather(tuesday,fair).
    weather(wednesday,fair).
    weather(thursday,overcast)
    weather(friday,rainy).
    weather(saturday,overcast).
    color(sky,blue,Day) if weather(Day,fair).
    color(sky,grey,Day) if weather(Day,overcast).
    happy(birders,Day) if weather(Day,fair) and
                          active(birds,Day).
    happy(birders,Day) if observed(rarebird,Day).
    active(birds,sunday).
    active(birds,tuesday).
    active(birds,thursday).
    observed(rarebird,wednesday).
    observed(rarebird,friday).
```

and ask our question again

```
Goal: happy(birders,When).
When = sunday
When = tuesday
When = wednesday
When = friday
When = tuesday
5 solutions
```

we have Tuesday reported to us twice, once by each of the two rules. There are two sets of requirements that both lead to the same conclusion. Turbo Prolog, following its top to bottom order, first found the rule about active birds and reported each day that met that requirement. Next, Turbo Prolog found the rarebird rule and reported days contingent on that. Tuesday met the requirements both times.

EXERCISES 3.4

Suppose you had a database which included:

```
clauses
    married(ann,abe).
    mother(ann,bet).
    mother(ann,cat).
    father(Man,Child) if married(Woman,Man) and
                          mother(Woman,Child).
    parent(Person,Child) if mother(Person,Child).
    parent(Person,Child) if father(Person,Child).
```

1. What will be Turbo Prolog's response to:

```
Goal: mother(ann,Whom).
Goal: father(abe,Whom).
Goal: parent(Who,bet).
```

2. Write queries to find out
   a) who is married to whom
   b) who has two parents known to the database

3.5 RECURSION

In addition to having rules that use other rules as part of their requirements, we can have rules that use themselves as part of their requirements. For example, suppose we have an automobile named Bessy that several people have owned.

```
owned(bessy,Person) if
                  bought(bessy,Person,Seller) and
                  owned(bessy,Seller).
```

This rule may be read as "A person owns the car, Bessy, if that person bought Bessy from someone and that someone was Bessy's owner." This kind of rule is called *recursive* because the relationship in the conclusion appears again (recurs) in the body of the rule, where the requirements are specified. Recursive rules are useful when a relationship carries from one object to the next and from that object on to another. In this case, ownership of Bessy moves from person to person. Our understanding of ownership passing along is expressed syntactically in the recurrence in the rule.

While the relationship appears both in the head and body of the rule, the objects, at least some of which are represented by variables, are different in the two places. The pattern of the relationship, moving from object to object, is defined by the way the variables in the rule are related. Notice the way the variables Person and Seller appear in different places in the rule above. The people represented by the variables take different roles in different parts of the rule.

A recursive rule is a way of generating a chain of relationships. For a recursive rule to be effective, however, there must be some place in this chain of relationships where the recursion stops. In our example, someone bought Bessy from the manufacturer.

```
owner(bessy,Person) if
                  bought(bessy,Person,manufacturer).
```

This stopping condition must be answerable in the database like any other rule. It can use other rules or facts, but should not use the recursive rule. Every time a recursive step along the chain is taken, some progress is made toward the stopping condition. In our example, each time we chain from a purchaser to the seller, we are getting closer to the original owner.

To specify a recursive rule for Turbo Prolog, we need a multiple rule definition. First we give the rule for the stopping condition and then the recursive clause. Occasionally, there will be more than one stopping condition. In those instances all the stopping rules should be written into the database before the recursive rule. Below is an example database and examples of questions and responses. Later (in Chapter 4) we will consider the process Turbo Prolog uses to keep track of the recursion. It is more important now to learn what Turbo Prolog does than to investigate the underlying process.

In the clauses section of this base, the first two lines make up the rule for ownership and the last four lines are facts.

```
clauses
   owned(bessy,Person) if
                  bought(bessy,Person,manufacturer).
```

```
owned(bessy,Person) if
                    bought(bessy,Person,Seller) and
                    owned(bessy,Seller).
bought(bessy,abe,ben).
bought(bessy,ben,carl).
bought(bessy,carl,fred).
bought(bessy,fred,manufacturer).
```

We can inquire about any one of these people owning Bessy.

```
Goal: owned(bessy,abe).
True
Goal: owned(bessy,sam).
False
```

Or we can present the more general question.

```
Goal: owned(bessy,Who).
Who = fred
Who = abe
Who = ben
Who = carl
4 solutions
```

Note the order in which these names appeared. Putting the stopping case first applies to the components of the multiple rule that defines the recursion; it is not a restriction on the ordering of the facts that the rule will use to reach its conclusions. The facts above could be in any order. For example,

```
bought(bessy,fred,manufacturer).
bought(bessy,ben,carl).
bought(bessy,abe,ben).
bought(bessy,carl,fred).
```

Whenever we ask for all the owners of Bessy, however, Fred will be reported first. His ownership is based on the first part of the rule, so it is verified first. The order in which the others will be reported will depend on their order in the base, not, say, on the order in which Bessy was acquired. Thus, using the order of facts in the second case above, the query and the response are

```
Goal: owned(bessy,Who).
Who = fred
Who = ben
Who = abe
Who = carl
4 solutions
```

Figure 3.3 contains another example with a recursive rule. The example is built on parent/child relationships. Family tree descriptions are some of the most

```
predicates
    mother(symbol,symbol)
    parent(symbol,symbol)
    ancestor(symbol,symbol)
clauses
    mother(ann,bet).
    mother(ann,cat).
    mother(bet,may).
    mother(may,nan).
    parent(Person,Child) if mother (Person,Child).
    ancestor(Person,Other) if parent(Person,Other).
    ancestor(Person,Other) if parent(Person,Middle) and
                              ancestor(Middle,Other).
```

FIGURE 3.3 Base and Rules for Ancestor

straightforward examples of Turbo Prolog recursion. They are common textbook examples because families are full of relationships that move from object (person) to object (person). Again, the non-recursive part of the rule for ancestor is specified before the recursive part of the rule.

```
Goal: ancestor(Older,Younger).
Older = ann,   Younger = bet
Older = ann,   Younger = cat
Older = bet,   Younger = may
Older = may,   Younger = nan
Older = ann,   Younger = may
Older = ann,   Younger = nan
Older = bet,   Younger = nan
7 solutions
```

EXERCISES 3.5

1. Add these three clauses and their supporting predicates to the database immediately above.

```
    married(abe,ann).
    father(Man,Child) if mother(Woman,Child) and
                         married(Man,Woman).
    parent(Person,Child) if father(Person,Child).
```

Now how will Prolog respond to

```
    Goal: ancestor(Older,Younger).
```

2. Sally invented a new game called Glump. She taught it to Joe, who taught it to Sam and May. May taught it to Leo and he, in turn, taught it to his sister. Write a database using a recursive rule that will tell us who knows how to play Glump.

3.6 POTENTIAL PROBLEMS WITH RECURSION

Sometimes in Turbo Prolog recursive rules do not result in the behavior we had planned. This misbehavior is not a result of providing the wrong rule; it has to do with the mechanism Turbo Prolog uses to try to arrive at conclusions from rules. You can avoid a number of problems by keeping in mind a few pointers for writing recursive rules.

One guideline has already been discussed: that the stopping case should be written first in the base. Because Turbo Prolog starts at the top of the database, putting the stopping case above the recursive rule ensures it will be tried before another step in the recursive chain is generated. When the end of the chain is reached, it will be noted and the recursion will be stopped, not by-passed.

A second guideline for more effective recursive rules is to put the recurring predicate at the end of the body of the recursive rule rather than at the beginning. This often helps contain the recursion on a narrower path, and sometimes is necessary if queries are going to be answered at all. When a recursive rule has the recurring predicate as the last part of the body of the rule, it is called *tail recursive* and the process, *tail recursion.*

For example, the recursive rule for ancestor that we used earlier could have been written with the recurring predicate first.

```
ancestor(Person,Other) if parent(Person,Middle) and
                           ancestor(Middle,Other).
ancestor(Person,Other) if ancestor(Middle,Other) and
                           parent(Person,Middle).
```

Either form will work for some queries. If we have a database using this second form, and make a query about all ancestors, however, the processing of this rule does not terminate correctly.

```
parent(ann,bet).
parent(bet,cat).
ancestor(Person,Other) if parent(Person,Other).
ancestor(Person,Other) if ancestor(Middle,Other) and
                           parent(Person,Middle).

Goal: ancestor(Older,Younger).
Older = ann   Younger = bet
Older = bet   Younger = cat
Older = ann   Younger = cat
```

```
----- Message -----
1002 Stack overflow
Press the SPACE bar
```

After the three correct answers, Turbo Prolog went into an endless circle between the two ancestor predicates in the recursive rule. The check for a parent fact is not inside the circle, so it could not indicate the stop. Before long, the space available in the computer was filled up with Turbo Prolog's records of the circles. At that point, the system refused to look further and stopped the execution.

Recursive rules that are written contrary to one or both of these two suggestions may still work correctly, at least for some kinds of queries. A request for all the values that a variable can take (for example, owned(bessy,Who).) is more apt to create a problem than a more specific request (for example, owned(bessy,abe).) The user needs to choose the way rules are written so that they match expected use of the rules.

Another potential source of problems with recursion can occur when the user did not mean to use recursion at all. If one rule has in its requirements the conclusion of a second rule, while the second rule has the conclusion of the first rule in its requirements, an oscillating recursion can be set up. For example,

```
brother(joe,ann).
brother(He,She) if sister(She,He).
sister(She,He) if brother(He,She).

Goal: sister(ann,Who).
Who = joe
Who = joe
Who = joe
Who = joe
(continues until stopped by CONTROL BREAK)
```

This base and request set up a cycle of rule calling upon rule that is fundamentally recursion, although it was not intended. The source of the problem in the base above is quite evident: brother is defined in terms of sister; sister is defined in terms of brother. In a larger, more complex world description where more than two definitions are involved in the cycle, it could be more difficult to discover.

The person defining rules should remain alert to the potential problems with recursion. There is always the possibility of the rules continuing to generate patterns that will not reach the stopping case. Continued generation of patterns like this is called infinite recursion. Programmers sometimes use infinite recursion on purpose but usually it appears by accident.

Recursion, however, provides a useful and powerful way of writing rules. Programmers use it regularly in describing the world in their Turbo Prolog database. In order to make writing recursive rules easier, recall the earlier discussion about writing any rule: it is often easier to write the rule if you focus on the way you would confirm that an object follows the rule than if you focus on trying to generate objects to meet the rule. Additionally, for writing recursive rules, use a two-step process. First, write the rule so that it is a correct definition, and then think about rearranging components to put them in the best order.

EXERCISES 3.6

1. Here is a set of clauses from an earlier base with some rules added. Turbo Prolog will not answer the query correctly. Why?

```
married(ann,abe).
mother(ann,bet).
mother(ann,cat).
mother(Woman,Child) if father(Man,Child) and
                         married(Woman,Man).
father(Man,Child) if mother(Woman,Child) and
                         married(Woman,Man).
parent(Person,Child) if mother(Person,Child).
parent(Person,Child) if father(Person,Child).
Goal: mother(ann,Whom).
```

2. What is a potential problem with this rule and how should it be corrected?

```
do(First_half,Second_half) if
        do(First_quarter,Second_half) and
        check(First_half,First_quarter).
```

SUMMARY

Rules can be added to facts in a database. The conclusion of a rule is in the rule's head and the requirements for the conclusion are in the rule's body. Rules can have constants and variables. The body of a rule may include a conjunction and may include the conclusion of another rule as part of its requirements. There may be more than one rule that specifies the same conclusion. In the case of recursion, there will usually be one that specifies the stopping case and one that gives the recursive rule. Careful choice and ordering of components in the body of the recursive rule, along with putting the stopping case first, will help guarantee that recursive rules behave as desired. •

SYNTAX SUMMARY

Rules

```
<conclusion> if <requirement1> and
        <requirement2> and ... and <requirementN>.
<conclusion> :- <requirement1>,
                <requirement2>,..,<requirementN>.
```

EXPERIMENTING WITH CHAPTER 3

Purpose:
    To see: adding rules to a base
            making queries based on rules
            interrupting processing

Rules are added to the database using the same mechanism as is used with facts, through the system's editor.

Adding rules requires two steps. The form of the rule's head, including the type of its objects, must be specified in the predicates section. The rules themselves must be entered in the clauses section. As you are editing your program, be sure to group together all the clauses with the same predicate name.

Start Turbo Prolog and go on to the main programming environment. Use the filer ("f") to load ("l" or just return) to retrieve an existing file from your disk, specifying its name. Use the editor ("e") to modify the program. As you are making modifications you may want to experiment with F5 (copy block), F6 (move block) and F7 (delete block) as well as other editor commands. Your Turbo Prolog manual contains tutorials and information about the editor and other parts of the programming environment.

When you have modified your program, you may want to save it. Use the filer to write your new program on the disk. The new program will replace the old one if you save it under the old name. If you give the new one a new name when saving it, the old one will not be lost. Be careful about choosing names that are too long. The first eight characters are the significant ones. Thus if you have a program named PROGRAM1.PRO and save one named PROGRAM11.PRO, the old one will be replaced and the new program saved under the shorter name.

By the time you are using rules, you may find you want to tell Turbo Prolog to stop what it is doing. This is particularly important if the system seems to be doing nothing for longer than the time it normally takes to respond or is continually repeating an answer. The process may have gone into an uncontrolled recursion. Telling Turbo Prolog to stop is called an *interrupt*. In Turbo Prolog ^BREAK (CONTROL and BREAK keys at the same time) will interrupt the execution and return to the "Goal:" state.

EXERCISES CHAPTER 3 ━━━━━━━━━━━━━━━━━━━━━━

1. Identify the Turbo Prolog concept or concepts described by each phrase below.
    a) The contents of a database.
    b) The two parts of a rule.
    c) The part of a rule containing the requirements component.
    d) When Turbo Prolog uses a rule, the first part that will be matched.
    e) The two ways objects can be represented in rules.

    f) The number of predicates in the head of a rule and the number in the body.

    g) Rules in which the predicate from the conclusion also appears in the requirements.

    h) The two parts that are almost always included in a recursive rule.

2. Using the database given below, select the number in front of the line or lines that show an example of the terms below.

```
[1] knows(sally) if knows(joe).
[2] knows(Hearer) if tells(Hearer,Teller) and
                            knows(Teller).
[3] tells(sue,sally).
[4] knows(joe).
```

    a) fact

    b) compound rule

    c) multiple rule

    d) recursive rule

    e) stopping case

    f) recursive case

3. Write Turbo Prolog databases to describe these situations.

    a) Shop at the grocery store that has the best vegetables.

    b) Shop at the market that has the lowest price on turkey.

    c) Shop at a store if it has good vegetables and beef on special.

    d) Shop at Ben's market.

    e) Four students saw the note Tom wrote to Joe. They sit in a row in class: Tom, Mary, Sally, Joe. Each one looked at the note before passing it on.

4

Turbo Prolog Processing

The purpose of this chapter is to help the learner:

- understand the sequence of steps Turbo Prolog uses to respond to a question.
- recognize which variables will be instantiated and in what order.
- define the scope of a variable.
- follow the pattern of Turbo Prolog's backtracking.

4.1 PROCESS

Up to this point, we have been focusing on *what* Turbo Prolog does. We have discussed the interaction between Turbo Prolog and the person using the language, observing the behavior that Turbo Prolog displays to the user. We have, however, briefly mentioned *how* Turbo Prolog does what it does. The system's processing was implied in our use of the term "pattern matching," and in noting that Turbo Prolog "goes to the top of the database" to begin a search for a fact or rule. Additionally, order in processing is implied by the recommendation to always have the stopping case for a recursion come "before" the recursive rule in the database. In this chapter, we will discuss these matters and some others that are affected by *how* Turbo Prolog does its work.

It is important to recognize that "what it does" and "how it does it" are two different ways to look at Turbo Prolog's processing (or any other processing, for that matter). Our fundamental goal is always to get Turbo Prolog to do what we want; in using the language, our primary focus is always on "what." In many cases, however, our knowing how Turbo Prolog is doing its work will help us to

51

build our database in a way that makes the system more effective and efficient. Additionally, something may go wrong so that the system does not behave as we want. Knowing some of the process Turbo Prolog is using may help us discover the reason for the problem.

Matching Facts and Questions

In its simplest form, a Turbo Prolog database consists of only facts. Recall that the general form of a fact is a predicate followed by one or more arguments in parentheses. In our simplest interaction, we present Turbo Prolog with a question that asks whether a fact is in the database. For example,

```
predicates
    weather(symbol,symbol)
clauses
    weather(sunday,fair).
    weather(monday,overcast).
    weather(tuesday,fair).
    weather(wednesday,fair).
    weather(thursday,overcast).
    weather(friday,rainy).
    weather(saturday,overcast).
```

Goal: weather(friday,rainy).

Turbo Prolog's task is to find the fact that matches the question. It begins at the top of the database (first fact entered), trying to match the predicate in the question with the predicate in the fact. It moves down the list of facts until it finds a matching predicate. Next, it checks all the arguments of the predicate to see if the ones in the question match with the ones in the fact. If all the arguments match, Turbo Prolog reports

    True

If, however, all the arguments in this fact do not match those in the question, Turbo Prolog continues its search. It goes to the next fact and tries again to find a predicate and a complete match. If it reaches the end of the base without finding a match, it reports

    False

Observing this process, we are reminded that a "False" response from Turbo Prolog means only that data in this base does not indicate a "True" answer.

EXERCISES 4.1 ━━━━━━━━━━━━━━

1. How many different facts can be matched in the database we were working with above?

2. If we add a fact to the database

    `weather(friday,fair).`

so that we have two facts of the form

    `weather(friday,<some>).`

how will Turbo Prolog treat this duplication?

4.2 GOALS WITH VARIABLES

When we use a variable, we are using a special name to stand in place of a specific object as an argument in a predicate. The name of the specific object is constant while the variable can name various objects. The variable name can stand for only one constant at a time.

To understand how Turbo Prolog uses variables, we have to differentiate between variables that have been associated with a specific constant name and ones that are in an unattached state, not currently associated with any one specific constant name. These two conditions are called

instantiated: the variable is associated with one specific constant name of an object.

uninstantiated: the variable is not currently associated with any specific constant name of an object.

The process of associating a variable with a specific constant is called *instantiation* of the variable. The terms *bound, free* and *binding* are often used as synonyms for these terms. In the Turbo Prolog manual, these terms are used.

Say we have a database of facts and ask a question with a variable name as an argument of the predicate.

    `Goal: weather(When,overcast).`

Turbo Prolog begins trying to match the predicate from the top of the database just as it did with a predicate with no variables. When it finds a fact with a matching predicate, it checks for a match in the arguments. If the number of arguments and all the constant arguments match, it instantiates the variable to the constant found in the corresponding position in the fact. The variable is instantiated with the constant that is the argument in the fact. Turbo Prolog then reports that instantiation to the user.

    `When = monday`
    `1 solution`

Turbo Prolog is reporting that the answer to the question is "True" if the variable is associated with the particular constant.

After reporting this instantiation to the user, Turbo Prolog continues its search for another fact that matches the question as stated. Turbo Prolog now uninstantiates the variable from the first constant and moves on down the database, looking for another match. This process of uninstantiating and looking further is called *backtracking*. It is called backtracking because Turbo Prolog "steps back" from an instantiation point to look for another possibility. Imagine that you need to close all the windows in a house, as in Figure 4.1.

You go in the outside door, decide to close the windows in room 1, close window A, close window B, choose room 2, close window D, close window C, choose room 4, choose room 3, close window E. Every time you back up to a decision point and move on to another choice of a window or a room, you are backtracking.

In processing a question, Turbo Prolog uses this kind of pattern. It continues backtracking and instantiating the variable, making as many matches as it can.

```
When = monday
When = thursday
When = saturday
3 solutions
```

When it reached the end of the base, Turbo Prolog reported the number of solutions it found. When Turbo Prolog finishes a searching cycle and returns to the prompt Goal:, all variables are uninstantiated. In fact, the variable name from the just-completed question no longer exists with any meaning to Turbo Prolog.

FIGURE 4.1 Backtracking in a House

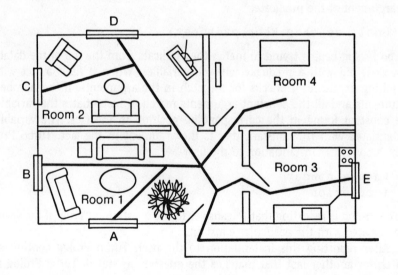

EXERCISES 4.2

For these exercises, refer to the weather database,
1. How many constants will be reported to
   Goal: weather(When,fair).
2. What will be the response to
   Goal: weather(friday,Outlook).

4.3 GOALS WITH MULTIPLE VARIABLES

The question we ask of Turbo Prolog may have more than one variable. In this case, it begins on its pattern matching task and follows the same process, instantiating all the variables in the specified question whenever it can match a fact. The instantiations are reported for each match.

```
Goal: weather(When,What).

When = sunday,      What = fair
When = monday,      What = overcast
When = tuesday,     What = fair
When = wednesday,   What = fair
When = thursday,    What = overcast
When = friday,      What = rainy
When = saturday,    What = overcast
7 solutions
```

Questions with Conjunctions

The questions we have looked at so far only contain one predicate. Turbo Prolog uses the same pattern matching process when presented with a question that contains a conjunction of predicates, such as

```
made_into(What,prunes) and made_into(What,wine).
```

Here we are asking for an instantiation of the variable, What, to a constant so that facts can be found that match both parts of the question.

Turbo Prolog matches the predicates left to right. It begins by treating the first predicate and its arguments as if it were a simple question. It looks through the database until it finds a matching fact and instantiates its variable or variables. Then it looks at the next predicate in the question. Any variable that was instantiated in the first match will have that value when the second match is started.

Now Turbo Prolog begins at the top of the database, treating this second predicate as an independent pattern to match, but with the instantiated variables treated as constants. It looks through the base, seeking a pattern that matches the second predicate. If it finds a match, instantiation is extended into these variables. This process continues through as many cycles as are needed to match all the parts of the question.

When Turbo Prolog can completely match all parts of the conjunction, it reports the instantiations. Then it goes on to try to make other matches using backtracking. First, it uninstantiates the variables in the match that was done last. In a compound question, this will be the component farthest to the right. It maintains the next-to-the-last instantiation and moves down through the database, looking for another match for the rightmost component, searching and matching to the bottom of the base. When potential matches for the last predicate are exhausted, Turbo Prolog steps back to the second-from-the-right component of the question and uninstantiates the variables there. Then it searches down the base, repeating the search, match and instantiate pattern.

Below is an example, which, for simplicity's sake, has only two components in the conjunction in the question. The process is the same for more components. The clauses in the database are numbered for reference in the process. In the extended description that follows, the indentation pattern shows the left-to-right and back-to-left processing of the components of the question.

```
predicates
   shade(symbol,symbol)
   color(symbol,symbol)
clauses
     1. shade(sox,black).
     2. shade(sox,red).
     3. shade(sox,green).
     4. shade(sox,white).
     5. color(shoes,black).
     6. color(shoes,white).
     7. color(sneakers,red).
     8. color(skates,white).
     9. color(running_shoes,black).
    10. color(boots,brown).
```

What footgear can I wear so that the shade of my sox matches the color of my footgear?

```
Goal: shade(sox,Hue) and color(Footgear,Hue).

Hue = black,   Footgear = shoes
Hue = black,   Footgear = running_shoes
Hue = red,     Footgear = sneakers
Hue = white,   Footgear = shoes
Hue = white,   Footgear = skates
5 solutions
```

Searching from the top, shade(sox,Hue) matches shade(sox,black) line 1

Hue is instantiated to black.

color(Footgear,Hue) becomes color(Footgear,black) for search.

Searching from the top for match to color(Footgear,black),
color(Footgear,black), matches color(shoes,black) line 5
Hue = black, Footgear = shoes reported,
Footgear uninstantiated, search continues at line 6
color(Footgear,black) matches color(running_shoes,black) line 9
Hue = black, Footgear = running_shoes reported,

Footgear uninstantiated, search continues at line 10

No more matches to color(Footgear,black), so backtrack.

Turbo Prolog steps back to the next component to the left
Hue is uninstantiated, search continues at line 2
Search is for a new match to shade(sox,Hue)
shade(sox,Hue) matches shade(sox,red) in line 2

Hue is instantiated to red.

color(Footgear,Hue) becomes color(Footgear,red) for search.

Searching from the top for match to color(Footgear,red),
color(Footgear,red) matches color(sneakers,red) line 7
Hue = red, Footgear = sneakers reported,

Footgear uninstantiated, search continues at line 8

No more matches to color(Footgear,red), so backtrack.

Turbo Prolog steps back to the next component to the left.
Hue uninstantiated, search continues at line 3
Search is for a new match to shade(sox,Hue)
shade(sox,Hue) matches shade(sox,green) in line 3

Hue is instantiated to green
color(Footgear,Hue) becomes color(Footgear,green)
Search is from the top for match to color(Footgear,green),
No match is found for color(Footgear,green), so backtrack.

Turbo Prolog steps back to the next component to the left.
Hue is uninstantiated
Search is for a new match for shade(sox,Hue) from line 4
shade(sox,Hue) matches shade(sox,white) in line 4

Hue is instantiated to white
color(Footgear,Hue) becomes color(Footgear,white)
Search begins at the top for match to color(Footgear,white),

color(Footgear,white) matches color(shoes,white) in line 6
Hue = white, Footgear = shoes reported,

Footgear is uninstantiated
Search for color(Footgear,white) continues at line **7**

color(Footgear,white) matches color(skates,white) in line **8**
Hue = white, Footgear = skates reported,

Footgear is uninstantiated
Search for color(Footgear,white) continues at line **9**

No more matches for color(Footgear,white) available, so backtrack.

Turbo Prolog steps back to the next component to the left.
Hue is uninstantiated
Search for new match to shade(sox,Hue) begins at line 5
No more matches for shade(sox,Hue) available, so backtrack.
No further components to the left, so Turbo Prolog reports
5 solutions

Notice that all the shade clauses came before the color clauses, and in the question, the shade component came before the color component. This is not necessary; they could appear in either order. The order in both the base and the question will, however, affect the order of the responses.

EXERCISES 4.3

1. Given the database above, what responses (in what order) would Turbo Prolog give to

        Goal: color(Footgear,Hue) and shade(sox,Hue).

2. If the base had been written using color as the predicate throughout (make shade into color) and asked

        Goal: color(sox,Hue) and color(Footgear,Hue).

    how would Turbo Prolog's answers be different, and why?

4.4 SCOPE OF VARIABLES

In a question with a conjunction, we usually have the same variable name in more than one place. When we are given an answer, that variable will be instantiated to the same constant throughout all parts of the question. The group of predicates where a variable name indicates the sharing of an instantiation is the *scope* of the variable. In the context of goals, the scope is from the prompt to the period at the end of the question.

When we begin another goal, the instantiations will not carry over, even if we are using the same variable name. Turbo Prolog has effectively forgotten the variable name. The scope of a variable cannot include separate goals. If we want

```
predicates
    weather(symbol,symbol)
    color(symbol,symbol,symbol)
    eyes(symbol,symbol)
    plan(symbol,symbol)
    ambivalent(symbol,symbol)
    skyeyes(symbol,symbol)
    happy(symbol,symbol)
    active(symbol,symbol)
    observed(symbol,symbol)
clauses
    (1)  weather(sunday,fair).
    (2)  weather(monday,overcast).
    (3)  weather(tuesday,fair).
    (4)  weather(wednesday,fair).
    (5)  weather(thursday,overcast).
    (6)  weather(friday,rainy).
    (7)  weather(saturday,overcast).
    (8)  color(sky,blue,Day) if weather(Day,fair).
    (9)  color(sky,grey,Day) if weather(Day,overcast).
    (10) eyes(grey,sue).
    (11) plan(picnic,sunday) if weather(sunday,fair).
    (12) ambivalent(birders,Day) if
                          weather(Day,rainy) and
                          active(birds,Day).
    (13) skyeyes(Person,Day) if color(sky,Hue,Day) and
                                    eyes(Hue,Person).
    (14) happy(birders,Day) if weather(Day,fair) and
                                active(birds,Day).
    (15) happy(birders,Day) if observed(rarebird,Day).
    (16) active(birds,sunday).
    (17) active(birds,tuesday).
    (18) active(birds,friday).
    (19) observed(rarebird,wednesday).
    (20) observed(rarebird,tuesday).
```

FIGURE 4.2 Rules Using Weather

to include more predicates in a variable's scope, we must combine all predicates in one query. In fact, this is why we use goals that contain conjunctions. Goals with just one predicate can give us only bottom-level answers when our database is made only of facts.

Rules

Queries using conjunctions become complex and tedious to ask. Even making use of the F8 key to reuse queries does not totally remove the problem of keying them in without typing errors. Using rules simplifies this situation. A rule is a definition that allows us to name one predicate in a goal in place of a complex conjunction of simple predicates.

It is not surprising, then, to find that Turbo Prolog treats rules very much like goals with conjunctions. When the pattern to be matched turns out to be a rule, the body of the rule is handled like a query. The variables in the head of the rule are instantiated to the same constants as the corresponding variables in the body. In rules, the scope of a variable includes all appearances in the head and the body within the rule. The following examples, which all use the database in Figure 4.2, show instantiation response patterns for rules, simple to complex. The clauses in the database are numbered for reference.

```
Goal: plan(picnic,sunday).
True

plan(picnic,sunday).                    found rule line 11
  weather(sunday,fair).                 found fact line 1
True

Goal: color(sky,blue,tuesday).
True

color(sky,blue,tuesday).                found rule line 8
  weather(tuesday,fair).                found fact line 3
True

Goal: color(sky,blue,When).
When = sunday
When = tuesday
When = wednesday
3 solutions

color(sky,blue,When).                   found rule line 8
  weather(When,fair).                   found fact line 1
  weather(sunday,fair).                 instantiate When
  When = sunday                         report
  weather(When,fair).                   found fact line 3
  weather(tuesday,fair).                instantiate When
  When = tuesday                        report
  weather(When,fair).                   found fact line 4
  weather(wednesday,fair).              instantiate When
  When = wednesday                      report
  weather(When,fair).                   no more matches
color(sky,blue,When).                   no more matches
3 solutions
```

```
Goal: color(sky,Hue,When).
Hue = blue,    When = sunday
Hue = blue,    When = tuesday
Hue = blue,    When = wednesday
Hue = grey,    When = monday
Hue = grey,    When = thursday
Hue = grey,    When = saturday
6 solutions
```

`color(sky,Hue,When)`	found rule line 8
`  color(sky,blue,When).`	instantiate Hue
`    weather(When,fair).`	found fact line 1
`    weather(sunday,fair).`	instantiate When
`    Hue = blue,   When = sunday`	report
`    weather(When,fair).`	found fact line 3
`    weather(tuesday,fair).`	instantiate When
`    Hue = blue,   When = tuesday`	report
`    weather(When,fair).`	found fact line 4
`    weather(wednesday,fair).`	instantiate When
`    Hue = blue,   When = wednesday`	report
`    weather(When,fair).`	no more matches
`  color(sky,blue,When).`	no more matches
`color(sky,Hue,When).`	found rule line 9
`  color(sky,grey,When).`	instantiate Hue
`    weather(When,overcast).`	found fact line 2
`    weather(monday,overcast).`	instantiate When
`    Hue = grey,   When = monday`	report
`    weather(When,overcast).`	found fact line 5
`    weather(thursday,overcast).`	instantiate When
`    Hue = grey,   When = thursday`	report
`    weather(When,overcast).`	found fact line 7
`    weather(saturday,overcast).`	instantiate When
`    Hue = grey,   When = saturday`	report
`    weather(When,overcast).`	no more matches
`  color(sky,grey,When).`	no more matches
`color(sky,Hue,When).`	no more matches

```
6 solutions
```

```
Goal: ambivalent(birders,When).
When = friday
1 solution
```

`ambivalent(birders,When).`	found rule line 12
`  weather(When,rainy).`	found fact line 6
`  weather(friday,rainy).`	instantiate When
`    active(birds,friday).`	found fact line 18
`When = friday`	report
`  weather(When,rainy).`	no more matches
`ambivalent(birders,When).`	no more matches

```
1 solution

Goal: skyeyes(Who,When).
Who = sue,   When = monday
Who = sue,   When = thursday
Who = sue,   When = saturday
3 solutions
```

`skyeyes(Who,When)`	found rule line 13
`  color(sky,Hue,When).`	found rule line 8
`    color(sky,blue,When).`	instantiate Hue
`      weather(When,fair).`	found fact line 1
`      weather(sunday,fair).`	instantiate When
`        eyes(blue,Who).`	no matches on second part of 13
`      weather(When,fair).`	uninstantiate When
`      weather(tuesday,fair).`	instantiate When
`        eyes(blue,Who).`	no matches on second part of 13
`      weather(When,fair).`	uninstantiate When
`      weather(wednesday,fair).`	instantiate When
`        eyes(blue,Who).`	no matches on second part of 13
`      weather(When,fair).`	uninstantiate When
`    color(sky,blue,When).`	no more matches
`  color(sky,Hue,When).`	found rule line 9
`    color(sky,grey,When).`	instantiate Hue
`      weather(When,overcast).`	found fact line 2
`      weather(monday,overcast).`	instantiate When
`        eyes(grey,Who).`	found fact line 10 on second part of 13
`Who = sue,   When = monday`	report (redo second part of 13)

`eyes(grey,Who).`	no more matches on second part of 13
`weather(When,overcast).`	found fact line 5 (redo rule in line 9)
`weather(thursday,overcast).`	instantiate When
`eyes(grey,Who).`	found fact line 10
`Who = sue,   When = thursday`	report (redo second part of 13)
`eyes(grey,Who).`	no more matches
`weather(When,overcast).`	found fact line 7 (redo rule in line 9)
`weather(saturday,overcast).`	instantiate When
`eyes(grey,Who).`	found fact line 10
`Who = sue,   When = saturday`	report (redo second part of 13)
`eyes(grey,Who).`	no more matches
`weather(When,overcast).`	no more matches
`color(sky,Hue,When).`	no more matches
`skyeyes(Who,When).`	no more matches
`3 solutions`	

EXERCISES 4.4

1. List the pattern of seeking and matching for the goal

   `happy(birders,When).`
2. How would the pattern of seeking and matching differ if the rule about skyeyes were

   ```
   skyeyes(Person,Day) if eyes(Hue,Person) and
                           color(sky,Hue,Day).
   ```

4.5 RECURSION

Recursion presents a special set of circumstances when we talk about how Turbo Prolog is doing its work. In recursion, the same rule is used over and over to work through the chain of relationships, finally reaching the stopping case. The process remains the same, however, with variables being instantiated and new patterns being set up for matching. The following examples use the database in Figure 4.3.

```
Goal: owned(bessy,fred).
True
```

`owned(bessy,fred).`	found rule line 1
`  bought(bessy,fred,manufacturer).`	found fact line 3

```
Goal: owned(bessy,ben).
True
```

`owned(bessy,ben).`	found rule line 1
`  bought(bessy,ben,manufacturer).`	no match
`owned(bessy,ben).`	found rule line 2
`  bought(bessy,ben,Seller).`	
`  bought(bessy,ben,carl).`	
`    owned(bessy,carl).`	found rule line 1
`      bought(bessy,carl,manufacturer).`	no match
`    owned(bessy,carl).`	found rule line 2
`      bought(bessy,carl,Seller).`	
`      bought(bessy,carl,fred).`	
`        owned(bessy,fred).`	found rule line 1
`          bought(bessy,fred,manufacturer).`	match 3

```
True
```

Note the separate instantiations of Seller. The scope of Seller in each use of the rule does not overlap the others. In the following example, lines marked -redo-show repeated attempts to match a predicate.

```
Goal: owned(bessy,Who).
Who = fred
Who = ben
Who = carl
3 solutions
```

`owned(bessy,Who).`	
`  bought(bessy,Who,manufacturer).`	
`  bought(bessy,fred,manufacturer).`	
`Who = fred`	
`  bought(bessy,Who,manufacturer).`	-redo-
`owned(bessy,Who).`	-redo-
`  bought(bessy,Who,Seller).`	
`  bought(bessy,fred,manufacturer).`	
`    owned(bessy,manufacturer).`	
`      bought(bessy,manufacturer,manufacturer).`	
`      bought(bessy,manufacturer,Person).`	
`  bought(bessy,Who,Seller).`	-redo-

```
    bought(bessy,ben,carl).
      owned(bessy,carl).
        bought(bessy,carl,manufacturer).
        bought(bessy,carl,Seller).
          bought(bessy,carl,fred).
            owned(bessy,fred).
              bought(bessy,fred,manufacturer).
Who = ben

  bought(bessy,Who,manufacturer).          -redo-
owned(bessy,Who).                          -redo-
  bought(bessy,Who,Seller).
  bought(bessy,fred,manufacturer).
    owned(bessy,manufacturer).
    bought(bessy,manufacturer,manufacturer).
    bought(bessy,manufacturer,Person).
  bought(bessy,Who,Seller).
      bought(bessy,carl,fred).
        owned(bessy,fred).
          bought(bessy,fred,manufacturer).
Who = carl

  bought(bessy,Who,manufacturer).          -redo-
owned(bessy,Who).                          -redo-
  bought(bessy,Who,Seller).
3 solutions
```

FIGURE 4.3 Owners of Bessy

```
predicates
   owned(symbol,symbol)
   bought(symbol,symbol,symbol)
clauses
   (1) owned(bessy,Person) if
                     bought(bessy,Person,manufacturer).
   (2) owned(bessy,Person) if
                       bought(bessy,Person,Seller) and
                       owned(bessy,Seller).
   (3) bought(bessy,fred,manufacturer).
   (4) bought(bessy,ben,carl).
   (5) bought(bessy,carl,fred).
```

EXERCISES 4.5

1. Trace the seek and match process for this base and goal to the point where one instantiation is reported.

```
clauses
    mother(ann,bet).
    mother(bet,may).
    parent(Person,Child) if mother(Person,Child).
    parent(Person,Child) if father(Person,Child).
    ancestor(Person,Other) if parent(Person,Other).
    ancestor(Person,Other) if
                              parent(Person,Middle) and
                              ancestor(Middle,Other).
    married(abe,ann).
    father(Man,Child) if mother(Woman,Child) and
                              married(Man,Woman).
    Goal: ancestor(Older,Younger).
```

2. Assume these two facts were added to the database just below the two existing facts named mother.

```
    mother(ann,cat).
    mother(may,nan).
```

What responses in what order would be reported to

```
    Goal: ancestor(Older,Younger).
```

SUMMARY

In addition to learning what Turbo Prolog does, we may want to know how it processes the user's requests. Turbo Prolog searches through its database, matching predicates and arguments from questions with predicates and arguments in the database. During matching, variables can be instantiated (if they have been matched with constants in the base) or uninstantiated (if they are currently unmatched). A variable's scope is the range over which an instantiation is shared. In Turbo Prolog, the scope is restricted to the clause in which the variable occurs. In questions or rules with conjunctions, the processing works left to right, successively matching predicates and instantiating variables. When Turbo Prolog is unable to match a predicate or is told to search further, the farthest-right match is undone and the process moves on from the last choice point. The pattern that Turbo Prolog uses, called backtracking, allows repeated search through the database for matches. •

EXPERIMENTING WITH CHAPTER 4

Purpose:

To see: how trace is used

a trace of a recursive rule

The Turbo Prolog programming environment includes a trace facility which can be used to observe the underlying pattern matching process taking place while a goal is being processed. (The discussion that follows is specific to the IBM-PC, but other implementations are similar.)

The trace window, which appears in the lower, right corner of the main programming environment screen, displays the predicate matches and variable instantiations. While the standard trace window can be used for observing a trace, it is easier to read if the window is expanded. To do this, choose Setup ("s") from the environment level, then use the down arrow to highlight "window size", key in return, use the down arrow to "trace window" and again key in return. Now hold down the shift key and use the left arrow to move the trace window about ⅔ of the way across the screen. Next, use the right arrow key (with no shift or other key) to expand the window toward the right to the edge of the screen. Use "ESC" to get out of Setup. When you trace a program, you will now have a larger window to observe. As you start the run process, the trace window will be hidden by the dialog window but will reappear for the trace.

To trace a program, you must first go into the editor (where your program should be loaded) and enter the key word "trace" at the beginning of your program. Now leave the editor and run the program, entering a goal. The first predicate to match will appear in the trace window. Uninstantiated variables will be indicated by an underscore, constants by words in quotation marks. Alternate choices remaining in the program are marked with an asterisk.

You can now make the program run one step at a time by repeatedly pressing the F10 key. As each step is made, the current goal or subgoal match being attempted in the program is indicated in the edit window by the cursor.

Figure 4.4 is an example of a screen showing a trace of

```
Goal: owns(bessy,carl).
```

Turbo Prolog provides alternatives in the tracing process that can be used to limit and focus the output of a trace. The Turbo Prolog manual lists and explains these options for specific machine implementations.

FIGURE 4.4 An Example Trace

```
  Run    Compile    Edit    Options    Files    Setup    Quit

                              Trace
Tra   CALL:  owned("bessy","carl")
pre   CALL:  bought("bessy","carl","manufacturer")
      REDO:  bought("bessy","carl","manufacturer")
      REDO:  bought("bessy","carl","manufacturer")
      FAIL:  bought("bessy","carl","manufacturer")
cla   REDO:  owned("bessy","carl").
      CALL:  bought("bessy","carl",_)
      REDO:  bought("bessy","carl",_)
      REDO:  bought("bessy","carl",_)
    RETURN:  bought("bessy","carl","fred")
      CALL:  owned("bessy","fred")
      CALL:  bought("bessy","fred","manufacturer")
    RETURN:  bought("bessy","fred","manufacturer")
    RETURN: *owned("bessy","fred")
    RETURN:  owned("bessy","carl")

Com
own
bou
bou
```

S-F9:Shift window   Arrows:Resizing   Any other key:End view

EXERCISES CHAPTER 4

1. Identify the Turbo Prolog concept or concepts described by each phrase below.
   a) The description of variables that depends on whether or not they are associated with a constant object.
   b) Stepping backward through a decision point to take a new path.
   c) In questions with conjunctions, the order in which predicates are matched.
   d) The effect on instantiation of a variable that appears more than once in a question with a conjunction.
   e) The range over which a variable refers to the same constant.
   f) The process during which rules are reused but the scope of the variables is separate.
   g) Recursive rules will process repeatedly until they reach this case.

2. Here is the clauses part of a database and three queries. In what order will the attempted matches be made for each question?

   ```
   carpet(green).
   chair(red).
   chair(green).
   pillows(white).
   pillows(green).
   Goal: carpet(Color) and chair(Color) and
                           pillows(Color).
   Goal: pillows(white) and carpet(Color) and
                           chair(Color).
   Goal: carpet(green) and chair(Color).
   ```

3. Write Turbo Prolog programs to provide
   a) A database with facts that describe your favorite books as funny, sad, science fiction and so on. Add rules that describe what to read in a certain mood.
   b) Write queries to get recommendations for reading based on your mood.
   c) Add the last week's weather day by day and a set of rules describing your mood based on weather conditions.
   d) Write queries to find out what to read on which day. If there could be several books appropriate for one day, try to predict the order in which they will appear.

5

Lists

The purpose of this chapter is to help the learner:

- understand the purpose of lists.
- write a Turbo Prolog program using a list.
- understand the head/tail notation.
- write list manipulation rules.

5.1 GROUPING INTO LISTS

In the world around us, we know about many specific objects. Humans, needing to simplify their thinking load, use an organizational tactic. We categorize a number of objects into a group, based on some characteristic the objects have in common. Then we are able to deal with the group instead of all the individual objects. In Turbo Prolog, the list is a similar mechanism. Lists are used to group objects together; then the list can be manipulated as a single object.

In Chapter 3, on rules, we had a database that included data about birders being happy when a rare bird was sighted. The information on bird sightings, however, is more apt to be a specific bird name, such as condor, than just "rarebird." We could write separate rules for each bird species considered rare, but this would be tedious and repetitive.

A better method in such circumstances is to have a list of the specific objects and to use items from the list when a particular object is needed. Thus, if we had a list of rare birds in a given area and time of year, and someone reported having seen, say, a western meadowlark, we could use Turbo Prolog to find out if that would make birders happy.

Syntax of Lists

All the objects we have seen so far have been simple objects. A list, however, is a compound object made of other objects, its components. The components of a list are commonly called elements.

To use a list in our Turbo Prolog programs, we will add another section to our program, the *domains* section. Like other program sections, this begins with its keyword, domains. The domains section precedes the predicates and clauses sections in the program. In the domains section we will establish the contents of the compound object we plan to use. Then we can use that object in our predicates section.

We will define a list to be made of zero or more symbols by using an asterisk. List is not a Turbo Prolog reserved word; it is one we have chosen to use here.

```
domains
    list = symbol*
```

A list itself in Turbo Prolog can be written in square brackets with commas between the list's elements. For example,

```
[condor,whooping_crane,seaside_sparrow]
```

If we put this into a database with the list as the argument of a predicate, our complete base looks like this:

```
domains
    list = symbol*
predicates
    rarebird(list)
clauses
    rarebird([condor,whooping_crane,seaside_sparrow]).
```

Now we are ready to consider the goal we want to use to find out about individual rare birds. We cannot simply ask

```
Goal: rarebird(condor).
```

because condor is a simple object, not a list. If we do give Turbo Prolog this goal, we will be told we have made a "type error".

If we use a general form query and ask

```
Goal: rarebird(What).
```

Turbo Prolog tells us

```
What = [condor,whooping_crane,seaside_sparrow]
```

That is, the variable What has been instantiated with the whole list as a single object. (Turbo Prolog includes quote marks around the element names. We will disregard them as they have to do with Turbo Prolog's internal representation of the objects, not the list structure.)

Since we want to get at the individual elements, we will write rules using a variable for each of the elements of the list. Each rule will specify a pattern with a variable in a specific location in the list. In the positions we are not concerned about, we will put an underscore. The underscore, remember, means "don't care". Thus, to write a rule that says a Bird is noteworthy if that Bird appears in the first position in our rarebird list, we will write the clause

```
noteworthy(Bird) if rarebird([Bird,_,_]).
```

By the same token, we will write two more rules, specifying that the Bird could appear in the second or third positions.

```
noteworthy(Bird) if rarebird([_,Bird,_]).
noteworthy(Bird) if rarebird([_,_,Bird]).
```

The predicates specification for these rules is

```
noteworthy(symbol)
```

as the rule has a simple object, not a list, in its head. The complete base now is:

```
domains
   list = symbol*
predicates
   rarebird(list)
   noteworthy(symbol)
clauses
   rarebird([condor,whooping_crane,seaside_sparrow]).

   noteworthy(Bird) if rarebird([Bird,_,_]).

   noteworthy(Bird) if rarebird([_,Bird,_]).
   noteworthy(Bird) if rarebird([_,_,Bird]).
```

Now we query

```
Goal: noteworthy(condor).
True
```

Condor was found as a noteworthy bird through the use of the first of the three rules. If we want to make changes in which birds are noteworthy, we can alter the base by simply changing the one predicate, rarebird, to one with a new list.

```
rarebird([cardinal,bluebird,meadowlark]).
noteworthy(Bird) if rarebird([Bird,_,_]).
noteworthy(Bird) if rarebird([_,Bird,_]).
noteworthy(Bird) if rarebird([_,_,Bird]).
```

This has gained us some flexibility, but not much, over having a separate fact for each bird. But meanwhile, we have added a constraint on our process, that it only handles lists of three birds. If we want to include more birds, we must write more noteworthy rules and alter the ones we have. Besides, the constraint on the number of elements in the list is not helpful; different size lists of birds are going to be needed.

EXERCISES 5.1

1. Write a Turbo Prolog notation for a list of the colors in the rainbow.
2. Write a predicate that has the list above as the argument for "rainbow."
3. Assuming the rainbow predicate is in a database, write a pair of queries that check to see which constant you chose for the seventh color in the rainbow, purple, violet or some other.

5.2 HEAD AND TAIL

We need a way of looking at the list, different from a "row of objects." Instead, we consider a list to be made of two parts; the *head*, which is the first element in the list, and the *tail*, which is a list of the rest of the elements. Note that the head is an element and the tail is a list. Because the tail is a list, it too has a head and tail.

LIST: [cardinal,bluebird,meadowlark]
HEAD: cardinal
TAIL: [bluebird,meadowlark]

LIST: [bluebird,meadowlark]
HEAD: bluebird
TAIL: [meadowlark]

LIST: [meadowlark]
HEAD: meadowlark
TAIL: []

The tail of the third example above is the special list, the *empty list*. It is a list like any other except that it is empty, so it does not have a head or a tail. (In Chapter 3, we discussed rules having a head and a body. The two uses of "head" are coincidental, not to be associated.)

A good model for this way of thinking of a list is a stack of cards, piled one on top of another placed in a box so that we cannot see any card except the top one. The top card is the head of the list, and the rest (everything below the head) is the tail.

If we remove the head from our stack of cards, we find ourselves once more with a stack that has a head and tail. The only difference is that our stack has become smaller. Repeating the removal of the current head eventually leads us to the bottom of the stack and an empty box. At this time, we must stop the process because the empty box has no head nor tail with which to continue. The head/tail relationship has moved down the stack of cards to a special case, the stopping place. Observe that this is a recursive pattern. To design a general method for accessing elements of lists, we will use recursion. Because the recursion continues as long as is necessary to reach the stopping case, we can use the method on lists of variable size.

First, however, we have to be able to separate the head and tail of a list. Turbo Prolog facilitates this with a special pattern for specifying head and tail, using a vertical bar and square brackets. For example,

```
[H|T]
```

Here H is the variable that represents the element that is the head of the list and T represents the list that is the tail of the list. The head and tail can be constants as well as variables. If we have

```
rarebird([cardinal,bluebird,meadowlark]).
```

in our database and ask

```
Goal: rarebird([H|T]).
```

Turbo Prolog responds

```
H = cardinal,  T = [bluebird,meadowlark]
1 solution
```

This special head/tail notation can only be applied at one level at a time. That is, one application of the notation only separates one item from the front of the list. To work further down the list we will use recursion to build specific rules.

EXERCISES 5.2

1. Identify the head and the tail of the following lists.
   ```
   [red,orange,yellow]
   [red,orange]
   [red]
   [ ]
   ```
2. Given a database including the clauses
   ```
   author([k_wilhelm,juniper_time,fault_lines]).
   author([u_leguin,left_hand_of_darkness]).
   ```
   what will be the responses to
   ```
   Goal: author([Head|Tail]).
   ```

3. Given a database with author predicates as above, write a query that would cause Turbo Prolog to report all author names (head of lists) without reporting the rest of the list.

5.3 MEMBERSHIP IN A LIST

We are now ready to write the rules that will allow us to find out if a particular name is included in a list. First, an element is a member of a list if it is the head of the list. We define this case in a fact with variables.

```
member(Element,[Element|_]).
```

If this not the case, then the element may still be a member if it is in the tail of the list. We define this case in a recursive rule.

```
member(Element,[_|Tail]) if member(Element,Tail).
```

The match will always be attempted with the head of the list. If no match is found there, the process moves on to the tail, treating it just like the original list, trying to match its head. Following the rule, Turbo Prolog now carries out its searching, using Tail as the list in the definition.

This multiple rule definition for membership,

```
member(Element,[Element|_]).
member(Element,[_|Tail]) if member(Element,Tail).
```

defines a recursive method for finding a specific element. The non-recursive part of the rule appears first, as it did with our earlier recursive rules. Say we make a query

```
Goal: member(a,[a,b,c]).
```

Turbo Prolog will answer "True" to this query because the element that is the head of the list matches the first argument of the first rule.

```
Goal: member(a,[b,a,c]).
```

will also be answered "True" because the second rule calls on the member rule recursively and thus moves down the list to check for a match.

What makes this recursion stop? There are two possibilities:

■ the match is found, as it was in the examples above, using the first (non-recursive) part of the multiple rule;

■ the match is never found because the name is not in the list.

If the name is not an element of the list, the recursion process will consider smaller and smaller lists until all that is left is the empty list, [ ]. Neither of our member rules say what to do with an empty list; it has neither head nor tail, so our rules do not apply. That is, a [ ] does not match either [Element | _] or [_ | Element]. Since there is no match to the empty list, the search is unsuccessful and the process stops.

The two stopping cases are expressed in our rules in different forms. The first case, where the name is found as the head of a list, is written explicitly in the rule as the first, non-recursive part of the definition. The second case, where the empty list is encountered, is implicit in the original specification, because the empty list has no head nor tail.

Note that the recursive process of looking for an element in a list does not actually modify the list in any way. It simply instantiates the variable, here named Tail, to successively smaller lists. The original list acts as the source for the smaller lists, but remains unchanged itself.

Look carefully at the first part of the membership rule.

```
member(Element,[Element|_]).
```

This is the first time we have seen a fact with variables rather than with constants. The fact shows the relationship between an object and the list of which the object is head. The relationship can be generalized over many lists, so a variable is used to stand in place of the object in the relationship, rather than a constant. This relationship is the conclusion of a rule; the requirements for the conclusion are embedded in the special notation for the head of a list, [H | _]. That is, using this notation is part of the definition of the requirements for the relationship.

Because the elements and the sublist are being represented by variables, they are affected by the same scope restrictions as the simple variables we saw earlier. That means, for example, that after completion of a goal like

```
Goal: rarebird([H|T].
H=cardinal, T=[bluebird,meadowlark]
```

both the H and T are once again uninstantiated.

EXERCISES 5.3

1. Given this database with these clauses plus the member rules,
   ```
   author([k_wilhelm,juniper_time,fault_lines]).
   author([u_leguin,left_hand_of_darkness]).
   author([l_m_alcott,little_women]).
   ```
   list all the responses to
   ```
   Goal: author(List) and member(Element,List).
   ```

2. What query will cause each of the lists to be reported as a unit (rather than as elements)?

5.4 USING MEMBERSHIP

To use the member rule and apply it specifically to the list of rare birds, we could use this database and ask questions.

```
noteworthy(Bird) if member(Bird,
              [condor,whooping_crane,seaside_sparrow]).
member(Element,[Element|_]).
member(Element,[_|Tail]) if member(Element,Tail).

Goal: noteworthy(condor).
True
Goal: noteworthy(robin).
False
Goal: noteworthy(Which).
Which = condor
Which = whooping_crane
Which = seaside_sparrow
3 solutions
```

A second way to build the rule will provide us with more flexibility. Instead of including the bird list in the noteworthy rule, we can use this form:

```
rarebird([condor,whooping_crane, seaside_sparrow]).
noteworthy(Bird) if rarebird(List) and
                    member(Bird,List).
member(Element,[Element|_]).
member(Element,[_|Tail]) if member(Element,Tail).
```

When we make the query

```
Goal: noteworthy(condor).
```

List is instantiated to the whole list in the rarebird predicate and then the membership predicate searches through the list for specific elements. This works as well as the earlier example and is somewhat more flexible, since only the rarebird list would require alteration to make changes. A second rarebird list could be added to expand the base. Turbo Prolog will process the lists as single objects, in order of their appearance in the base.

```
rarebird([condor,whooping_crane, seaside_sparrow[).
rarebird([bluebird,cardinal]).
noteworthy(Bird) if rarebird(List) and
                    member(Bird,List).
member(Element,[Element|_]).
member(Element,[_|Tail]) if member(Element,Tail).

Goal: noteworthy(What).
What = condor
```

```
What = whooping_crane
What = seaside_sparrow
What = bluebird
What = cardinal
5 solutions
```

There is, however, a risk in this structure whether it has one list or more. The critical condition is in the noteworthy rule. The rule is actually made of two parts: one instantiates List; the other checks for membership in List. Our rule must contain the predicate that instantiates List first, and then the predicate that checks for membership in the list. If, in the noteworthy rule, we had put the member predicate before the predicate that instantiates the List, some queries would not be processed correctly. The rearranged rule, named not_worthy, is shown in the database below, along with the same member rule and one of the rarebird lists.

```
rarebird([condor,whooping_crane, seaside_sparrow]).
not_worthy(Bird) if member(Bird,List) and
                    rarebird(List).
member(Element,[Element|_]).
member(Element,[_|Tail]) if member(Element,Tail).
```

If we run a program with this kind of rule in it, Turbo Prolog will give us a warning about it. If we overrule the warning (using F10) we can still process some goals.

In response to a query about a specific bird, Turbo Prolog behaves correctly, but if we ask Turbo Prolog to specify all the birds that the base considers not_ worthy, it goes out of control.

```
Goal: not_worthy(What).
What = condor
What = whooping_crane
What = seaside_sparrow
```

Rather than telling us that there are no more members of the list, Turbo Prolog continues looking for others until we interrupt by keying ^ break (CONTROL BREAK). If we observe Turbo Prolog's processing, we will see the pattern being used. In the following description, variables that start with V represent elements, and variables that start with T represent the tail of a list. The first part of the description, through the point where condor is reported, is complete. After that point, only the form of the predicate that is to be matched to the rarebird predicate is shown in the example.

```
Goal: not_worthy(What).
not_worthy(What) ?
member(What,List) ?
```

```
member(What,[What|T1])
rarebird([What|T1]) ?
rarebird([condor,whooping_crane,seaside_sparrow])
not_worthy(condor)

What = condor

rarebird([V2,What|T2]) ?

What = whooping_crane

rarebird([V2,V3,What|T3]) ?
What = seaside_sparrow

rarebird([V2,V3,V4,What|T4]) ?
rarebird([V2,V3,V4,V5,What|T5]) ?
rarebird([V2,V3,V4,V5,V6,What|T6]) ?
rarebird([V2,V3,V4,V5,V6,V7,What|T7]) ?
  (^break here interrupted the process)
```

Turbo Prolog returns the names from the list, in order, as it should. Then, having been asked to find another, it goes on creating longer and longer lists of variables, looking for a list in the base that might match. Not surprisingly, this search is persistently unsuccessful.

Turbo Prolog's left-to-right processing means that the member requirement of the not_worthy rule is being processed before the list has been instantiated. To write more effective rules, have the list instantiation first (as it is in the noteworthy rule) and the membership processing second. This ordering makes intuitive sense in this problem so the programmer would probably have written the correct "noteworthy" form in the beginning. In general, however, first drafts of rules may not be in optimal order. A typical programmer, writing rules, will specify the requirements and then rearrange the form for improved effectiveness.

EXERCISES 5.4

1. Given these clauses

```
author([k_wilhelm,juniper_time,fault_lines]).
author([u_leguin,left_hand_of_darkness]).
author([l_m_alcott,little_women]).
member(Element,[Element|_]).
member(Element,[_|Tail]) if member(Element,Tail).
```

what will be Turbo Prolog's response to

```
Goal: author(List) and member(juniper_time,List).
Goal: author(List) and member(u_leguin,List).
```

```
Goal: author(List) and member(little_women,List).
```

2. Given these clauses

```
dwarves([sleepy,grumpy,happy,sneezy,
                          dopey,bashful,doc]).
no_beard([bashful,snow_white]).
member(Element,[Element|_]).
member(Element,[_|Tail]) if member(Element,Tail).
```

write a rule that will specify which dwarves have no beard.

3. Based on the description of the behavior of the not_worthy rule, you should be able to predict the responses to the query following this base, which has two rarebird lists in it. What will be the responses?

```
rarebird([condor,crane,sparrow]).
rarebird([cardinal,bluebird]).
not_worthy(Bird) if member(Bird,List) and
                    rarebird(List).
member(Element,[Element|_]).
member(Element,[_|Tail]) if member(Element,Tail).
Goal: not_worthy(What).
```

5.5 PROCESSING LIST ELEMENTS

In addition to checking to see if an element is a member of a list, we might be interested in the element in a special location. The element in the front of the list is easy, as that is the head of the list.

```
front(Element,[Element|_]).
```

Finding the last element of a list requires working our way recursively to a single-element list.

```
last(Element,[Element]).
last(Element,[_|Tail]) if last(Element,Tail).
```

Other, intermediate positions from the front can be specified by using a hybrid pattern, combining the "elements in a row" way of thinking with the "head/tail" way of handling lists of various sizes. Notice that the description of Turbo Prolog's processing of the not_worthy rule used this form. The first locations are specified and the remainder is allocated to the tail. For example,

```
third_place(Element,[_,_,Element|_]).
```

If we use the third place rule on a list that is not long enough to have a third place, Turbo Prolog will simply respond "no solution".

Another question we might ask is about successive elements. We can inquire about two elements being next to each other somewhere along the list.

```
next_to(First,Second,[First,Second|_]).
next_to(First,Second,[_|Tail]) if
                            next_to(First,Second,Tail).
```

The following is an example that shows the use of these rules for inquiring about particular elements in a program that includes the rarebird lists.

```
rarebird([condor,whooping_crane, seaside_sparrow]).
rarebird([bluebird,cardinal]).

front(Element,[Element|_]).

last(Element,[Element]).
last(Element,[_|Tail]) if last(Element,Tail).

third_place(Element,[_,_,Element|_]).

next_to(First,Second,[First,Second|_]).
next_to(First,Second,[_|Tail]) if
                            next_to(First,Second,Tail).
```

The query below is looking for the first bird in each rarebird list.

```
Goal: rarebird(List) and front(Element,List).
List = [condor,whooping_crane,seaside_sparrow],
Element = condor
List = [bluebird,cardinal],
Element = [bluebird
2 solutions
```

The next query is looking for the last bird in each list.

```
Goal: rarebird(List) and last(Element,List).
List = [condor,whooping_crane,seaside_sparrow],
Element = seaside_sparrow
List = [bluebird,cardinal],
Element = cardinal
2 solutions
```

This next query returns the third bird in the list. Since one list has only two birds, it has no third bird; the only response is from the longer list.

```
Goal: rarebird(List) and third_place(Element,List).
```

```
List = [condor,whooping_crane,seaside_sparrow],
Element = seaside_sparrow
1 solution
```

This last query reports pairs of birds that are next to each other in the lists.

```
Goal: rarebird(List) and next_to(One,Two,List).
List = [condor,whooping_crane,seaside_sparrow],
One = condor,
Two = whooping_crane

List = [condor,whooping_crane,seaside_sparrow],
One = whooping_crane,
Two = seaside_sparrow

List = [bluebird,cardinal],
One = bluebird,
Two = cardinal
3 solutions
```

EXERCISES 5.5

1. Given these facts:
   ```
   author([k_wilhelm,juniper_time,fault_lines]).
   author([u_leguin,left_hand_of_darkness]).
   author([l_m_alcott,little_women]).
   ```
   which rule from this section could you use to find out if any author has more than one book listed?

2. Write a rule using a rule from the rarebirds database that reports all author names (heads of list) in response to the query
   ```
   Goal: author_names(Which).
   ```

3. In Exercises 5.1, you wrote two queries to test whether the last color in a predicate named rainbow was violet or purple. Rewrite those queries using rules from this section.

5.6 PROCESSING LISTS

Besides checking on the elements in lists, we often want to manipulate or build lists. To build a list, we can start with elements or we can start with lists to be combined into one larger list. First, we will discuss a method for combining lists into a larger list, called appending. Append is not built into Turbo Prolog, so we will define it here.

Appending one list to another is a way of constructing a new list from two other lists. *Appending* means that the third, combined list is made up of the first list with the second list added on to its end. This is accomplished recursively, with the recursive rule working down the first list, associating the successive head elements with elements in the equivalent position in the combined list.

```
append([Element|List1],List2,[Element|List3]) if
                        append(List1,List2,List3).
```

When the recursion reaches the end of the first list, the whole second list is added as the tail of the third list.

```
append([ ],List,List).
```

To visualize appending, consider again the stack of cards representing a list, as in Figure 5.1. To append two stacks of cards, first take cards from the first stack, one at a time from the top, and suspend them over the place the combined list will be stacked. When the whole of the first list is suspended, move the second list as a unit to the place where the combined list will be stacked. Then, unsuspend the elements above and let them settle into the combined, final list.

The first list being empty is the stopping case for the recursion. The rule combining the two cases is

```
append([ ],List,List).
append([Element|List1],List2,[Element|List3]) if
                        append(List1,List2,List3).
```

FIGURE 5.1 Appending Two Stacks of Cards

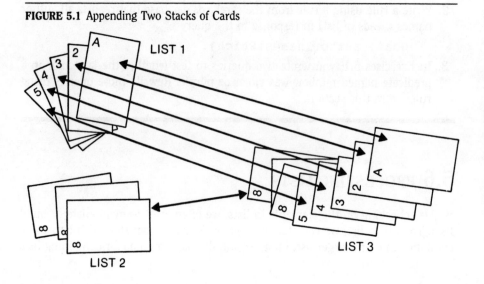

```
Goal: append([x,y,z],[a,b,c],Result).
Result = [x,y,z,a,b,c]
```

```
Goal: append([a,b,c],[c,d,e],Result).
Result = [a,b,c,c,d,e]
Goal: append(a,[a,b,c],Result).
2206 Type error
```

This did not append because the first argument is an element, not a list.

```
Goal: append([ ],[a,b,c],Result).
Result = [a,b,c]
```

The empty list is a list so append works here.

Append can be used to find component lists as well as the combined list. Turbo Prolog can accept variables for any of the three lists that appear in the append predicate. This flexibility and power is available because the rules define the relationship without regard to which lists are known or unknown.

```
Goal: append([x,y,a],List,[x,y,a,b,c]).
List = [b,c]
Goal: append(List,[a,b,c],[x,y,a,b,c]).
List = [x,y]
```

Another analogy that may help you visualize these recursive definitions is that of a jointed telescope. Each time the append rule is used, imagine another sliding tube is extended. The tubes are collapsed at the completion of the process, when matching variables are instantiated. We could draw these two examples as telescopes (see Figures 5.2 and 5.3).

```
Goal: append([x,y,a],List,[x,y,a,b,c]).
```

FIGURE 5.2 Telescope of Determining List2

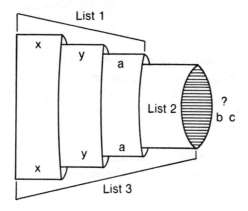

```
Goal: append(List,[a,b,c],[x,y,a,b,c]).
```

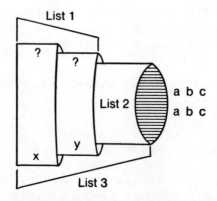

FIGURE 5.3 Telescope of Determining List1

We can also use append to find all the possible sublists that would make up a combined list.

```
Goal: append(List1,List2,[a,b,c]).
List1 = [ ],
List2 = [a,b,c]
List1 = [a],
List2 = [b,c]
List1 = [a,b],
List2 = [c]
List1 = [a,b,c],
List2 = [ ]
4 solutions
```

As we see these lists and sublists being generated, we might expect them to have attained a sort of permanent status. However, the names of these lists are variables and they obey the same scope rules we saw earlier. After the completion of a goal, all the variables lose their instantiations. A goal might use append to create a list from two others, but when the goal is complete, that combined list no longer exists.

We can use append in other list manipulation by including append within the scope of other rules. For example, to reverse a list,

```
reverse([ ],[ ]).
reverse([Head|Tail],List) if
                    reverse(Tail,Result) and
                    append(Result,[Head],List).
```

This particular version of reverse, while simple to understand, has some problems. We have two rules of thumb about arranging the order of requirements components in a rule. One is that tail-recursion is preferred. The second is that predicates with fewer alternatives (like reverse) should be specified first.

Because of these conflicts, some patterns of use for the rule will cause Turbo Prolog to give you warnings about uninstantiated variables. These warnings can be over-ridden with the F10 key.

The rule above can reverse either way. That is, the first argument can be known and the second found, or the second known and the first found. With one pattern, nothing unusual happens.

```
Goal: reverse([a,b,c],What).
What = [c,b,a]
1 solution
```

With the opposite argument pattern, however, first we are given a warning that a variable in append is uninstantiated. If we over-ride the warning, we get one correct solution. Then Turbo Prolog backtracks looking for other solutions, gradually filling up the available space in the computer.

```
Goal: reverse(List,[a,b]).
List = [b,a]
-----------Message-----------
 Press space bar to continue
----------------------------
```

The problem results from trying to find more than one reverse when there is only one. In Chapter 6 we will learn how to solve this problem.

Using this rule and others in this base, we can write a rule about palindromes, which are strings of letters that are the same frontward and backward. (This rule only handles palindromes with double center letters.)

```
palindrome(List1,List2) if
                    append(List1,List3,List2) and
                    reverse(List1,List3).

Goal: palindrome([a,b,c],Result).
Result = [a,b,c,c,b,a]

Goal: palindrome(Half,[a,b,c,c,b,a]).
Half = [a,b,c]
```

EXERCISES 5.6 ━━━━━━━━━━━━━━━━━━━━━━━━━━━━━

1. Given this database

```
rarebird([condor,crane,sparrow]).
rarebird([bluebird,cardinal]).
append([ ],List,List).
append([Element|List1],List2,[Element|List3]) if
                        append(List1,List2,List3).
reverse([ ],[ ]).
reverse([Head|Tail],List) if
                    reverse(Tail,Result) and
                    append(Result,[Head],List).
palindrome(List1,List2) if
                    append(List1,List3,List2) and
                    reverse(List1,List3).
```

what will be the response to

```
Goal: rarebird(List) and
            append([frigate_bird],List,Result).
Goal: rarebird(List) and
            append(What,[cardinal],List).
Goal: rarebird(List) and
            append(List,List,Result).
Goal: rarebird(L1) and rarebird(L2) and
            append(L1,L2,Result).
```

2. Given the database above, what will be the response to

```
Goal: rarebird(List) and reverse(List,Result).
Goal: rarebird(List) and palindrome(List,Result).
Goal: rarebird(List) and palindrome(Half,List).
```

3. Write a rule that will create a palindrome without duplicating the last element in the source list. For example,

```
odd_pal([a,b,c],Result).
Result = [a,b,c,b,a]
```

━━

5.7 EXTENDING COMPOUND OBJECTS

The lists we have seen are one type of compound object. Each list is made up of a series of objects called elements. All elements in a list must be the same kind of object, but the number of elements within the list may vary. We can extend the flexibility of lists by using more complex objects for the elements. For example, the elements themselves can be lists.

```
domains
    e_list = symbol*
    list = e_list*
predicates
    one(symbol,e_list,list)
```

With this definition, we now have the predicate "one" that requires a simple symbol for its first argument, a list of zero or more symbols for its second argument, and a list (which also may be empty) made up of symbol lists for its third argument.

There is a second way to define compound objects in which the objects are nested rather than lined up sequentially. The inner objects are defined in the form of a predicate and its objects.

```
domains
    teacher = name(symbol,symbol)
predicates
    two(teacher)
clauses
    two(name(prolog,rogers)).
```

This mechanism allows structures to be treated as units or to be disassembled into individual objects.

This mechanism also allows us to specify options for the same compound object. By extending the domains specification, we can use the same predicate for a variety of forms of structure. The optional forms are listed and separated by semicolons.

```
domains
    teacher = name(symbol,symbol); tutor(symbol)
predicates
    two(teacher)
clauses
    two(name(prolog,rogers)).
    two(tutor(joe)).
```

These forms of domains definitions can be combined to design very flexible compound objects.

```
domains
    list = symbol*
    item = s(symbol); l(list)
    item_list = item*
predicates
    three(item_list)
clauses
    three([l([a,b,c]),s(dog),s(cat)]).
```

EXERCISES 5.7

1. Which of the following clauses would be legal for arguments in predicate "three" above?

   a) `three([s(dog)]).`
   b) `three([s(dog),l([dog])]).`
   c) `three([]).`
   d) `three(l[]).`
   e) `three([s(dog,cat)]).`

2. Using the original clause for "three" in the text above, how will Turbo Prolog respond to these goals?

   ```
   Goal: three(What).
   Goal: three([_,What,_]).
   Goal: three([_,_,s(What)]).
   ```

SUMMARY

Turbo Prolog lists provide a mechanism for grouping objects. Lists are made up of elements; in Turbo Prolog we need to be able to manipulate both the lists as wholes and the individual elements in the lists. Individual elements can be accessed either through their position in the list or by using the head/tail separation of the list which allows access to the first element of a specified list. A list either has a head and tail or else it is the special, empty list.

Recursion provides the basis for list processing tools, such as membership in a list, appending of lists and analysis of lists for particular elements. •

Syntax Summary

```
empty list []
list [Element1,Element2,..ElementN]
head/tail  [Head|Tail]
    head is an element
    tail is a list
```

hybrid form (enumerating some elements and a tail)

```
[Element1, Element2,...|Tail]
```

```
domains
    <list> = <element-domain>*
    <type> = p(domain); q(domain);...
```

EXPERIMENTING WITH CHAPTER 5

Purpose:
To see: different instantiation patterns in rearranged predicates
comparisons of efficiency for different patterns

Processing patterns and relative efficiency of different predicate arrangements can be seen by using trace during queries. Output from using the trace directive is shown below. It indicates the amount of work Turbo Prolog must do to process different queries. The goals in the first set show that the number of attempted matches for finding solutions will depend on the balance of different predicates in the base and on the order in which compound goals are presented. If the predicate with fewer choices appears first, less work is required.

The base being used:

```
trace
predicates
   shade(symbol,symbol)
   color(symbol,symbol)
clauses
   shade(sox,black).
   shade(sox,green).
   shade(sox,white).
   shade(sox,red).
   color(shoes,black).
   color(sneakers,red).
```

```
Goal: shade(sox,Hue) and color(shoes,Hue).
CALL:     shade(sox,_)
RETURN:   *shade(sox,black)
CALL:     color(shoes,black)
RETURN:   color(shoes,black)
Hue = black
REDO:     shade(sox,_)
RETURN:   *shade(sox,green)
CALL:     color(shoes,green)
REDO:     color(shoes,green)
FAIL:     color(shoes,green)
REDO:     shade(sox,_)
RETURN:   *shade(sox,white)
CALL:     color(shoes,white)
REDO:     color(shoes,white)
FAIL:     color(shoes,white)
REDO:     shade(sox,_)
RETURN:   shade(sox,red)
CALL:     color(shoes,red)
```

```
REDO:     color(shoes,red)
FAIL:     color(shoes,red)
1 solution

Goal: color(shoes,Hue) and shade(sox,Hue).
CALL:     color(shoes,_)
RETURN:   color(shoes,black)
CALL:     shade(sox,black)
RETURN:   shade(sox,black)
Hue = black
1 solution
```

In the next set, the predicates appear in equal numbers. The different goal forms show that putting the predicate with fewer variables first cuts down on the processing involved.

The base used is:

```
trace
predicates
    shade(symbol,symbol)
    color(symbol,symbol)
clauses
    shade(sox,black).
    shade(sox,green).
    color(shoes,black).
    color(sneakers,red).

Goal: shade(What,Hue) and color(shoes,Hue).
CALL:     shade(_,_)
RETURN:   *shade(sox,black)
CALL:     color(shoes,black)
RETURN:   color(shoes,black)
What = sox,  Hue = black
REDO:     shade(_,_)
RETURN:   shade(sox,green)
CALL:     color(shoes,green)
REDO:     color(shoes,green)
FAIL:     color(shoes,green)
1 solution

Goal: color(shoes,Hue) and shade(What,Hue)
CALL:     color(shoes,_)
RETURN:   color(shoes,black)
CALL:     shade(_,black)
RETURN:   shade(sox,black)
Hue = black,  What = sox
1 solution
```

EXERCISES CHAPTER 5 ▬▬▬▬▬▬▬▬▬

1. Identify the Turbo Prolog concept or concepts described by each phrase below.

   a) An ordered sequence of constants, variables or lists.
   b) The repetition process that is the basis for many predicates that process lists.
   c) Why using the head/tail notation for lists is more flexible.
   d) In a rule like append, which of the arguments may be the unspecified argument when the process is begun.
   e) Two ways lists may be accessed.
   f) A way individual elements in a list can be specified.

2. Each of the next 5 questions gives a Turbo Prolog sentence followed by several statements. For each question find ALL the statements that are true about the Turbo Prolog sentence.

   a) `carpet(hall,beige).`
   1) This is a rule.
   2) This is a fact.
   3) This could be the stopping condition for recursion.
   4) This uses list notation.

   b) `need_ice if weather(warm) and picnic(Day).`
   1) This is a rule.
   2) This is a fact.
   3) This could be the stopping condition for recursion.
   4) This uses list notation.

   c) `classes([german,physics,calculus,composition]).`
   1) This is a rule.
   2) This is a fact.
   3) This could be the stopping condition for recursion.
   4) This uses list notation.

   d) `owned(Property,Person) if`
                       `bought(Property,Person,builder).`
   1) This is a rule.
   2) This is a fact.
   3) This could be the stopping condition for recursion.
   4) This uses list notation.

   e) `classes([H|Tail]).`
   1) This list could contain 2 elements.
   2) This list could contain more than 2 elements.
   3) This list could contain 0 elements.
   4) This list could contain 1 element.

3. Write Turbo Prolog programs for these problems.

   a) Write a database that includes several lists as arguments to the predicate "trip". Each list should specify the streets you travel on a specific trip around your town.

b) Write rules and queries that will find out if you use the same street as part of two trips.

c) Write a new database for palindrome that makes palindromes with an uneven number of elements, but instead of modifying palindrome, modify reverse so that the reversed component is one shorter than the original.

d) Write a database that has a rule which accepts a list and two elements as arguments. The rule should go through the list and replace every occurrence of the first element with the second element. That is:

```
Goal: swap(a,z,[a,b,a,c],New_list).
New_list = [z,b,z,c]
```

II

Advanced Topics

How Turbo Prolog Is Like and Unlike Other Languages

PROGRAMMING CONCEPTS

Being fluent in one programming language usually helps a person in learning another language. However, some people who have experience in computer programming find that this prior experience interferes to some degree with their learning of Turbo Prolog. While many of the concepts these programmers already know, such as system organization and file handling, are helpful, other concepts are not. Two facets of the programmers' prior knowledge create problems:

1. their model of what a program is
2. the components they expect to find making up the language.

95

THE PROGRAM MODEL

Procedural Model

The model that these programmers have learned (and been taught) is "the program as recipe." In this model, the program is an algorithm that specifies carefully and explicitly the steps the computer must take to create a result. Results, be they intermediate or final, are recorded in the computer memory in labelled locations, which are called variables. The programmer's responsibility consists of specifying the correct sequence of steps and being sure that correct values are stored under correct variable names. This model, which is called the von Neumann model, is useful for programming in procedural languages, such as Pascal, BASIC and C.

Declarative Model

Programming requirements are different, however, for a declarative language. The primary responsibility of the declarative programmer is to give a correct definition of the problem and its components. The definition is made up of facts and rules. Each fact or rule is a logical sentence that makes an assertion about the problem. Output is generated when a query is made of the facts and rules. The output is derived from the definition. The system, not the explicit instruction of the programmer, controls the processing that produces the output. Most current declarative languages are versions of Prolog. Turbo Prolog is one of the newest members of the Prolog family.

Program Processing

Say, for example, one were designing a program module to search a group of records to find the last name of a person whose first name is Mary and who lives in Austin. In Turbo Prolog, such a program might contain a set of facts of the following form.

```
person(mary,bain,dallas).
person(mary,jones,austin).
person(john,jones,austin).
person(mary,smith,austin).
```

The facts are a part of the program rather than a separate component called "data." That is, the program is the database and vice versa. The facts would be used along with an interactive query of the form:

```
Goal: person(mary,Last_name,austin).
```

This would precipitate the response

```
Last_name = jones
Last_name = smith
2 solutions
```

The response returns constant values (marked by beginning with a lower-case letter) that, when used in place of the variable (upper-case letter) in the question, yield statements true according to the base. The list of facts and the question are the totality of this Turbo Prolog program. Rules, which appear in the database along with the facts, are another component of Turbo Prolog programs. Rules contain a head and a body, separated by the composite symbol, colon-dash, or the word "if". The head of the rule expresses a conclusion and the body of the rule specifies the condition or conditions required for the conclusion. Rules typically include variables. For example,

```
schedule(skiing,Month) :- winter(Month)
```

This rule could be read "Schedule skiing during a month if that month is in the winter".

Pattern Matching

A program comparable to the example above might be written in Pascal using records. Assuming the records are stored in an array, the search module might look like this:

```
Procedure Find(Base:DataArray;
               Var Sought:LastNameType);
Var Index:Integer;
Begin
  Index := 1;
  While NOT(Base[Index].FirstName=Mary
        AND Base[Index].Local=Austin) Do
    Index := Index + 1;
  Sought := Base[Index].LastName
End;
```

The specific directions that the Pascal programmer gives in the program instruct the system to look through the records one by one until the matching record is found. When using Turbo Prolog, this kind of search for a matching pattern is implicit, and is, in fact, the basis for all Turbo Prolog programs. Components of a Turbo Prolog program are general record structures. Under Turbo Prolog's control, the search for matching patterns proceeds through the records from the top to the bottom of the database. The Turbo Prolog programmer exerts some control over the processing by choosing the order of the components in the database. If, in the above Turbo Prolog example, the fourth line had come first, order in the result returned would have been different.

```
Last_name = smith
Last_name = jones
2 solutions
```

There are some special extensions to the logical core of Turbo Prolog that programmers can use to add a more procedural flavor to a program. Fundamentally, however, a Turbo Prolog program does not express the procedural "Do this" but rather says "This is what's known; this is what the answer should look like; find it."

LANGUAGE COMPONENTS

Variables and Values

In the Pascal example above, several of the instructions are assignment statements. The Pascal programmer specifies when values will be stored in variables. The assignment statement is a fundamental part of procedural languages and one that experienced programmers expect to find in a programming language.

The pattern-matching process in Turbo Prolog also involves the association of specific constant values with individual variable names (called instantiation), but again it is Turbo Prolog rather than the programmer who directs it. Thus, there is no assignment statement in Turbo Prolog. Values and variables are associated by their matching in patterns. There are some supplements to the core Turbo Prolog language that allow programmers to effect assignments, but again these are beyond the descriptive core of Turbo Prolog. Rather than simple assignments, they are ways of building Turbo Prolog structures.

Turbo Prolog, unlike most other versions of Prolog, includes strong typing of its variables. In this way, Turbo Prolog is like modern imperative languages such as Pascal and Ada. The argument types, including structured types, are declared in the domains section and the predicate forms are declared in the predicates section. Several standard simple variable types (symbol, integer, real, string and char) are available.

Control Statements

The second component that programmers expect to find in a language are control statements. In the Pascal program above, the While..Do loop controls iteration. Instructions for looping, conditionals and transfer to subroutines appear in procedural languages. The transfer of control that these instructions accomplish in procedural programming is built into the Turbo Prolog system. Thus, conditionals and loops do not appear in Turbo Prolog programs as they do in procedural languages. Alternate choices are accomplished through failure and backtracking. Repeated application is accomplished through backtracking and recursion.

Alternation

For example, one might have two rules defining a comfortable place to live.

```
comfortable(Place)  :- climate(Place,hot),
                              house(Place,airconditioned).
comfortable(Place)  :- climate(Place,moderate).
```

The rules can be read

1. A place is comfortable if the climate there is hot and the house there is air-conditioned.
2. A place is comfortable if the climate there is moderate.

Both these rules would be in the database at the same time. Multiple rules defining the same outcome provide alternatives. In this case, rule 1 or rule 2 can be used to determine that a place is comfortable.

During Turbo Prolog's pattern-matching process, the rules are checked in the order they are listed. If the conditions in the first rule are not true, the system backtracks to try the next rule. This mechanism allows complex conditionals to be expressed, with the multiple rule form providing an easy-to-under stand specification.

If no rule succeeds, the Turbo Prolog system reports the failure. Failure of rules allows for negation in a Turbo Prolog program. It is only negation within the facts and rules provided in the program. Turbo Prolog assumes that the given program contains all true assertions; this is called the closed-world assumption.

Repetition

Recursion is frequently used in Turbo Prolog. Its structure can be built with multiple rules, including one or more stopping cases and one or more recursive cases. For example,

```
ancestor(Older,Younger)  :- parent(Older,Younger).
ancestor(Older,Younger)  :- parent(Older,Middle),
                              ancestor(Middle,Younger).
```

These two rules can be tested and used repeatedly for matching because the scope of a variable is limited to the sentence in which it appears. Turbo Prolog recognizes tail-recursion and optimizes it into iteration. Thus, where appropriate, efficiency can be improved without requiring the programmer to build the iterative structure.

Rules, single or multiple, can be used both to check (confirm the truth of) a fact or to generate values that are confirmed in the facts. Thus, the multiple rule shown above (along with related facts in the database) could be used to confirm

```
Goal: ancestor(adam,bob).
```

to find an ancestor

```
Goal: ancestor(Who,bob).
```

to find a descendant

```
Goal: ancestor(adam,Who).
```

or to generate through backtracking all ancestor-descendant pairs

```
Goal: ancestor(Senior,Junior).
```

Note that, unlike procedure parameters in many languages, the variables are not limited to being either input or output parameters. In most Turbo Prolog definitions, any parameter can take the role of input or output. However, rule definitions may be processed more efficiently for some input/output patterns than others.

LISTS

Turbo Prolog has special pattern notation for list structures, which, combined with backtracking and recursion, provides convenient list manipulation. The notation is

```
[Variable1|Variable2].
```

where Variable1 is the first element in the list (the head), Variable2 is a list of the remaining elements (the tail), and the square-bracketed structure is the whole list. Thus the list constructor and the list selector are implicit within the pattern. For example,

```
append([ ],List,List).
append([Element|List1],List2,[Element|List3]) :-
                          append(List1,List2,List3).
```

This append rule can be used to combine two lists into one, to break one list into all its component-list-pairs, or to return or confirm a sublist. In processing a complex set of specifications, Turbo Prolog attempts its matches left to right through the rule. Procedural programmers, accustomed to concerning themselves about sequence of processing, tend to assume that one component must be "completed" before processing can move on. Turbo Prolog does not require instantiation of all variables in one component before proceeding to the next. Rather, Turbo Prolog returns the most general match that meets the current specificatons.

CALCULATIONS

Turbo Prolog can be used to do arithmetic. For example, the factorial function can be represented recursively.

```
factorial(0,1) :- !.
factorial(N,Value) :- PreN = N-1,
                      factorial(PreN,Subvalue),
                      Value = Subvalue*N.
```

While Turbo Prolog can do both integer arithmetic and real arithmetic, declarative programming is not convenient for "number crunching." The special operator =, which allows a form of assignment is an extra-logical feature. It requires there be no uninstantiated variable in the expression to its right, so rules using it are limited in the roles of input and output parameters. The rule above will work for

```
Goal: factorial(3,Value).
```

but not for

```
Goal: factorial(N,6).
```

Using arithmetic to derive information from a database is a more appropriate Turbo Prolog task than is generating numeric values. For example, given a database with facts about individuals' birth dates, one could write a rule like

```
can_vote(Person) :- birthyear(Person,Year),
                    Age = (1986 - Year),
                    Age >= 18.
```

VIEW OF PROGRAMMING

Logic and Control

Most experienced programmers, learning declarative programming and therefore having to alter their view of what progamming means, typically choose one of two images. The first is to view a declarative language as "higher-level" language in which specifications are turned into the actual "program" by the system. The second view recognizes that, while some programs are algorithms, not all need be. Declarative programs are theorems, specifying known rules and facts. When a query is made in the program, an additional clause is combined with the theorem and a proof is generated. The proof is what produces the answer to the query.

In either of these views, control in the program is separated from the logical component. In a program, the knowledge of relationships and outcomes is its logical component. The directions expressing the process for using this knowledge to find a problem solution make up the control component. The declarative programmer's central concern is to express the logical component. When this has been done, modifications can be made for improving process performance without invalidating the logic component. This separation of logic and control has two advantages:

1. The cognitive load on the programmer is reduced, so that original programs can be written with less time and effort.
2. The logic component, being free of control information, is easy to read and understand, providing the attendant advantages of improved correctness, maintainability and reuse.

Program Development

Turbo Prolog allows development of program units for subproblems of a task. Design and testing of modules is facilitated by Turbo Prolog's interactive programming environment. Turbo Prolog also supports modularity so the mechanisms for encapsulation and other software engineering techniques are available.

For further reading on these topics, see Backus [1978], Kowalski [1974b] and Warren, Pereira and Pereira [1977], listed in Appendix B.

6

Improving the Efficiency of Turbo Prolog Programs

The purpose of this chapter is to help the learner:

■ understand the different views of
  descriptive or declarative semantics.
  prescriptive or procedural semantics.
■ recognize the control mechanisms in Turbo Prolog.
■ consider alternatives that improve efficiency of Turbo Prolog programs.
■ understand and be able to use the cut in modifying control.

6.1 DESCRIPTIVE VERSUS PRESCRIPTIVE

In the beginning of this book, we discussed a Turbo Prolog program as a base of facts and rules that describe a world. The facts and rules specified things that are true in that particular world. Queries made of the database asked Turbo Prolog to derive conclusions about the world, or to provide us with object names that made a particular statement true. When we take this view of a Turbo Prolog program, we are looking at the *declarative* or *descriptive* semantics (meaning) of the program.

In Chapter 4, we focused on the process Turbo Prolog uses to analyze the questions and the database. In answering our questions, we saw that the system follows a sequence of steps, matching predicates and arguments, instantiating variables and backtracking when necessary. If we extend our thinking along this line, we can view a Turbo Prolog program as a series of directions to Turbo Prolog, telling it how to go about discovering the answer to our query. The way we write our rules and questions affects the process Turbo Prolog will follow. The programmer becomes a direction-giver rather than a world-definer. When we look at a Turbo Prolog program as a set of instructions to be carried out, we are considering the *procedural* or *prescriptive* semantics of the program.

In looking at the prescriptive semantics of a program, we are recognizing that the program will be processed by Turbo Prolog on a machine. As part of the processing, the system uses methods that the programmer knows about and takes advantage of. For example, matching starts at the top of the database, predicates in rules are attacked left-to-right, and backtracking takes up where it left off, uninstantiating variables. The programmer builds on these methods to write a program that will behave effectively.

The facet of a program that concerns how a program will work is called *processing control* or simply *control*. As we have seen, control in a program depends on both the system (with its underlying machine) and the order of the program components which the programmer specifies.

In considering efficiency for a Turbo Prolog program, we must recognize that we are looking at the prescriptive, not the descriptive semantics of the program. Meanwhile, the descriptive view of the program should not be forgotten, as it is of fundamental importance in logic programming. One of the advantages of Turbo Prolog programming, however, is that we can consider the logic and the control in a program as separate matters. The descriptive semantics of a program refers to the analysis of the problem to be solved. The prescriptive semantics refers to the processes by which the problem is to be solved. Conceptually, the Turbo Prolog programmer is concerned with the descriptive semantics; practically, the programmer must also be concerned with prescriptive semantics.

As an example of descriptive versus prescriptive semantics, consider the multiple rule for appending lists that we saw in Chapter 5. First, recall the idea: append means that the combined list will be made of the first list with the second list added on at the first list's end. We recognize that in the special case where the first list is empty, the combined list will be just the same as the second list. We also see that in the general case, the element that is the head of the first list will be the head of the combined list and that the tail of the first list with the second list appended to it will be the tail of the combined list. We wrote the Turbo Prolog rules for this definition. (Note: from here on, we will use the terse forms of ":-" for "if" and "," for "and".)

```
append([ ],List,List).
append([Element|List1],List2,[Element|List3]) :-
                    append(List1,List2,List3).
```

Descriptively, we can see that this rule gives us a definition of what append means. The two rules describe the two cases: when the first list is empty; when the first list is not empty (and therefore has a head and tail). Between the two parts, the relationship append is totally defined.

In contrast, looking at append prescriptively, we must consider a sequential process that consists of copying constant values from one list to another. Consider the case where list1 and list2 are given and the combined list is being created. The elements from the first list are copied into the combined list, one at a time in order. When all of list1 has been copied, list2 is copied as a whole on the end of the partially built combined list.

Consider the second case, where list1 and the combined list are known and list2 is being found. Elements in list1 and the combined list are matched from the beginning of the lists until all of list1 has been matched. Then the rest of the combined list is copied as list2.

In the third case, where list2 and the combined list are known, list1 will be created. Elements from the combined list are skipped over until the remainder of the combined list matches list2, then the elements that have been skipped over are copied into list1.

Notice that to consider the append process prescriptively, one must think about the different cases separately. The descriptive view covers all three cases because the rules express the definition of the relationship.

Goals

Like the append example, any Turbo Prolog rule can be read two ways: as a description of relationships between objects, or as a prescription for carrying out some task.

When we ask a question, we are setting up a *goal* for Turbo Prolog to try to satisfy. The goal it is processing has been *activated*. Descriptively, this goal asks the program to confirm that the relationship in the query is true in the world description that the database represents, or in the case of a query with variables, report variable instantiations that satisfy the goal. Thus, if Turbo Prolog is able to find facts and rules that allow the conclusion in the goal, we can say the goal is *satisfied* or that it has *succeeded*. If a particular goal cannot be satisfied, that goal has *failed*.

While trying to satisfy a goal, Turbo Prolog is often required to establish intermediate goals. These goals are activated in turn as processing continues. When the goal that Turbo Prolog is trying to satisfy is the head of a rule, the requirements in the body of the rule must be met. Thus these one or more components become intermediate goals or *subgoals* of the head goal.

When a particular goal has been satisfied, it has been matched or *unified* with a fact, or with the head of a rule in which the subgoals have been satisfied. The unification may later be rejected when failure of another goal causes backtracking. For example,

```
shade(sox,green).
shade(sox,black).
color(shoes,black).
color(shoes,white).
```

```
mono_feet(Hue) :- shade(sox,Hue),
                      color(Footgear,Hue).
Goal: mono_feet(Tone).
```

First, mono_feet is matched to the head of the rule. Since Tone and Hue both are variables, no instantiations to constants are done. Rather

```
shade(sox,Hue).
```

is taken as a subgoal and a search for its match is started. It matches with

```
shade(sox,green).
```

This subgoal is now satisfied and Hue is instantiated to green. Turbo Prolog's processing moves to the right in the rule and a new subgoal is set up

```
color(Footgear,green).
```

The search through the database does not find a match for a color predicate with green as the second object, so the goal fails.

The failure of the second subgoal forces Turbo Prolog to backtrack, giving up the match and instantiations from the success of the first subgoal. It searches on from the place of the rejected unification, trying to *re-satisfy* the first subgoal in the rule.

In this case, the next unification of

```
shade(sox,Hue).
```

will instantiate Hue to black, and the goal

```
color(Footgear,black).
```

will succeed with Footgear instantiated to shoes.

Since both the subgoals in the rule have succeeded, the original goal

```
mono_feet(Tone).
```

has also succeeded, and the instantiation

```
Tone = black
```

will be reported and backtracking begins again. Another match is sought for

```
color(Footgear,black).
```

but re-satisfying this goal fails. Backtracking releases the instantiation of Hue to black and Turbo Prolog tries to re-satisfy the earlier goal

```
shade(sox,Hue).
```

This also cannot be satisfied, so there are no more ways the goal

```
mono_feet(Tone).
```

can succeed with the rule we have been using. A further search finds no more ways for mono_feet to possibly succeed, so Turbo Prolog reports

```
1 solution
```

In introducing the idea of goals which succeed or fail, we are revisiting the concepts that were discussed in Chapter 4. There we talked about the methods that Turbo Prolog uses to respond to our queries. Here again we are talking about the methods it uses. The difference between these two discussions lies in our perspective on the Turbo Prolog program.

In Chapter 4, our view of a program was strictly as a definition. The facts and rules we provided described a complete world and specified what was true in that world. There, our view of Turbo Prolog's processing was that Turbo Prolog, in responding to our query, had to follow certain methods to discover correct responses to give us.

When we speak of processing goals in Turbo Prolog, we are taking a more dynamic view of a program. We view the process Turbo Prolog uses to get from our query to its responses as a path to be traveled, with goals and subgoals as milestones along the path. Each goal must be activated and Turbo Prolog succeeds or fails in attaining the goals along the path. For example, to return to the database above

```
shade(sox,green).
shade(sox,black).
color(shoes,black).
color(shoes,white).
mono_feet(Hue) :-shade(sox,Hue),
                 color(Footgear,Hue).
```

As shown in Figure 6.1, we could diagram the goals and subgoals from the earlier example of mono_feet(Hue).

FIGURE 6.1 Goals and Subgoals in mono_feet(Hue).

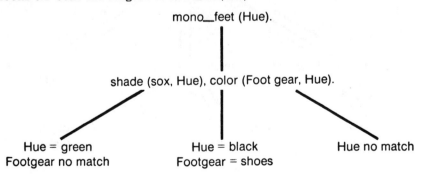

Using a diagram such as this, we can trace attempts at meeting goals by moving down in the diagram and trace backtracking by moving up. A similar diagram, with the addition of arrows, shows the path that Turbo Prolog follows in processing the goals. In this format, the whole process of the earlier example would look like Figure 6.2.

Parallelism

The diagram in Figure 6.2 points out another characteristic of a Turbo Prolog program. We have been assuming that a computer under Turbo Prolog's control will be doing only one thing at a time; it will be following a single path attempting to succeed at a sequence of goals. In our diagram, this path starts at the top and goes down branches, starting with the ones shown to the left. The place where facts appear in the diagram is determined by where they appear in the database.

In looking for any (or all) possible instantiations for Hue, however, there is no reason for investigation of the middle path in the diagram to wait until the first path is done. These paths could be traveled in parallel. To process a declarative program in parallel requires that the underlying language/computer system be different from that we have been discussing. Parallel Prolog systems are an important area in research and development. Several of the articles and books listed in Appendix B discuss this topic further. Considering such systems is beyond the scope of this book, but every Turbo Prolog programmer should be aware of the inherent parallelism in a declarative program.

FIGURE 6.2 Processing Pattern for mono_feet(Hue).

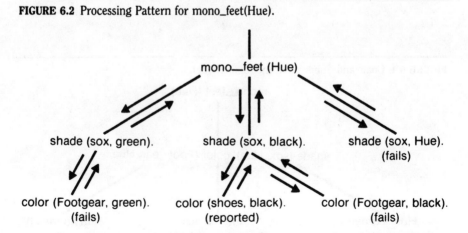

EXERCISES 6.1

1. Write two brief paragraphs, one which explains this program descriptively, and one which explains it procedurally.

```
reverse([ ],[ ]).
reverse([Head|Tail],List) :-
                    reverse(Tail,Result),
                    append(Result,[Head],List).
append([ ],List,List).
append([Element|List1],List2,[Element|List3]) :-
                    append(List1,List2,List3).
```

2. Draw a diagram of the processing pattern for this base and query.

```
loud(sirens).
loud(music).
can_buy(house).
can_buy(music).
Goal: can_buy(What),loud(What).
```

6.2 PROCEDURES

An even more process-oriented view of a Turbo Prolog program is to consider each rule in a program as a *procedure* that outlines the activity that will be carried out in finding an answer. The answer will be in the form of a value (object) for a variable. If a rule has the head of a second rule in its body, the procedure calls on the second rule as a subprocedure.

When a procedure calls a second procedure, it can give the second procedure some already instantiated variables and can get back from the second procedure instantiations for more variables. With Turbo Prolog procedures, variables can have values sent along when a procedure is called or returned from the called procedure. In the vocabulary of procedures, these values are called *parameters*. They can be specific values or uninstantiated variables.

This view of a Turbo Prolog program is extremely prescriptive. It sees a program as a recipe or algorithm that specifies the behavior of the computer under control of a program. This view of a program disregards the descriptive component of the program.

Logic Plus Control

A Turbo Prolog program that is going to be carried out on a computer has both descriptive and prescriptive semantics. The descriptive semantics consists of the facts and rules, and the meaning to the programmer of the description of the problem. The prescriptive semantics is built from the programmer's awareness of how the Turbo Prolog system will process the program it is given and from the choices the programmer makes in the expression and ordering of facts and rules.

A Turbo Prolog program is written descriptively so that the logic can be checked and correctness assured. The meaning of the program can be understood without regard to how the system will properly carry out the program. Then the same program can be considered prescriptively to be sure the realities of the system will properly carry out the program. Here, too, efficiency in time and space for computing can be considered. The program can be modified to improve its behavior as long as the logical correctness remains. That is, the prescriptive semantics changes while the descriptive semantics remains unchanged.

Earlier, in Chapter 4, we discussed a few rules of thumb for avoiding some problems with recursion and for improving efficiency. One of those rules suggested putting the recursive component as far right in a definition as possible. That is

```
<predicate> :- <some constraint>,
               <predicate with different variables>.
```

Descriptively, this definition has the same meaning in whichever order the requirements components appear. The definition can be written either way and analyzed to be sure it is a correct definition. If the definition is going to be used on a computer, pragmatic concerns arise and the definition must be viewed prescriptively. At this time, the programmer must choose a specific order for the components.

Another suggestion for limiting the work Turbo Prolog must do was to arrange components in the body of a rule so that the predicate that appears first is the one with the fewest possible matches. That is, if the goal is to have matching shoes and sox out of three pair of shoes and twenty pair of sox, it is usually better to choose a pair of shoes and then search for matching sox than to start with the sox. That is, you would ask the question

```
Goal: color(shoes,Hue), shade(sox,Hue).
```

if you have fewer predicates that specify the color of shoes and use

```
Goal: shade(sox,Hue), color(shoes,Hue).
```

if you have fewer predicates about the shade of sox. Again, the definition of matching shoes and sox does not depend on the order, but it may be important practically for Turbo Prolog. It means that fewer false starts at matching the complete rule will be processed.

Another place where rule structure affects Turbo Prolog's efficiency is in the direction of use of a definition. Descriptively, a definition can specify results in any argument location. For example,

```
ancestor(Oldperson,Youngperson) :- ...........
```

can be used to find Oldperson if Youngperson is given

```
Goal: ancestor(Who,jean).
```

or to find Youngperson when Oldperson is given

```
Goal: ancestor(george,Who).
```

Depending on how the definition of ancestor is written, one of these requests is apt to require a lot more work of the computer than the other. If the Turbo Prolog programmer knows the predicate will be used primarily one way, then the definition can be put in order to cater to that use.

For similar reasons, other definitions of predicates may be written to narrow the use of predicates to only the tasks they do efficiently. Another predicate, descendant, could be defined that works more efficiently when the Oldperson is specified and the Youngperson sought. In building related definitions like these, however, one should carefully avoid building an unwanted oscillating recursion.

EXERCISES 6.2

1. Write two definitions of ancestor that are descriptively valid, choose one as prescriptively preferable and explain why.
2. Write the clauses section of a database of four facts, a rule for ancestor and a rule for descendant.

6.3 CUT

Turbo Prolog has a special goal called the cut that can be used to modify the prescriptive semantics of a Turbo Prolog program. The *cut*, which is written !, is a special goal; when activated, it succeeds immediately but only once. If backtracking causes processing to return to the cut, the cut will not only fail but will cause the failure of its parent goal. The *parent goal* is the goal that called the rule in which the cut appeared. For example,

```
holiday(tuesday,july_4).
weather(tuesday,fair).
weekend(saturday).
weekend(sunday).
make(potato_salad,Day) :- picnic(Day).
picnic(Day) :- weather(Day,fair), !,
                weekend(Day).
picnic(Day) :- holiday(Day,july_4).

Goal: make(potato_salad,tuesday).
False
```

In processing this query, Turbo Prolog sets up the goal of finding a match for the predicate in the question. It finds the match in the rule where it instantiates Day to tuesday. This next goal activated requires Turbo Prolog to find a match for

```
picnic(tuesday).
```

Turbo Prolog makes the match to the first rule that has picnic(Day) as its head. Its subgoal

```
weather(tuesday,fair).
```

is activated and succeeds. Moving right,

```
!
```

is activated and succeeds immediately. Next

```
weekend(tuesday).
```

is activated. This goal fails, so backtracking is begun. The backtracking moves to the goal

```
!
```

which, having succeeded once, now fails. At the same time it also fails the parent goal, which is

```
picnic(tuesday).
```

Since this goal fails,

```
make(potato_salad,tuesday).
```

also fails and Turbo Prolog reports "False".

Notice that there was another rule in the database with picnic(Day) as its head. We can see that this rule would have confirmed tuesday as a day to make potato salad if the Turbo Prolog processing had used this rule. Because of the cut, this rule will not be used. The backtracking to the cut will cause the failure of the parent goal

```
picnic(tuesday).
```

and no further attempts at matching will be made.

The cut provides a way of modifying the behavior of Turbo Prolog as it processes its goals. The cut is used in conjunction with the other means the programmer has to control behavior: the order in which facts, rules and predicates in rules are written. These control mechanisms have meaning only in the procedural semantics of Turbo Prolog. They have no meaning in the declarative semantics.

By modifying the database above, we can gain more insight into how cut affects Turbo Prolog's behavior. First, we will add fair weather for the weekend and remove all cuts from the base.

```
holiday(tuesday,july_4).
weather(tuesday,fair).
weather(saturday,fair).
weather(sunday,fair).
weekend(saturday).
weekend(sunday).
make(potato_salad,Day) :- picnic(Day).
picnic(Day) :- weather(Day,fair), weekend(Day).
picnic(Day) :- holiday(Day,july_4).

Goal: make(potato_salad,When).
When = saturday
When = sunday
When = tuesday
3 solutions
```

In tracing the goals generated by the query, we can see that only one, early instantiation of When was unsuccessful. Using the first picnic rule, When was instantiated first to tuesday, but then the facts did not meet the requirements for that picnic rule. That rule was used for saturday and sunday. Tuesday was then reported because of the second picnic rule.

To see the effects of cut, we will now modify the first picnic rule to its earlier form.

```
picnic(Day) :- weather(Day,fair), !,
               weekend(Day).

Goal: make(potato_salad,When).
No solution
```

This time we have asked Turbo Prolog to give us any instantiation for When rather than asking for confirmation as we did in the first example. Nonetheless, tuesday is the first instantiation made to the variable, When. The backtracking to the cut caused failure of goals clear back to the original

```
make(potato_salad,tuesday).
```

so "no solution" is reported.

Next, we will modify the first picnic rule so that the cut is furthest right in the body of the rule.

```
picnic(Day) :- weather(Day,fair),
               weekend(Day), !.
Goal: make(potato_salad,When).
When = saturday
1 solution
```

In answering our query this time, Turbo Prolog attempted to satisfy the goals in the rule with When instantiated to tuesday as before. This time, however, the goal

```
weekend(tuesday).
```

failed and caused backtracking before the cut was reached. Because the cut had not been activated, Turbo Prolog could backtrack and find the new instantiation for When, saturday. The goal

```
picnic(saturday).
```

succeeded through the three subgoals of the rule, including the cut, so Turbo Prolog reported

```
When = saturday
```

Looking for other solutions, Turbo Prolog backtracked. Working back from the right in the body of this rule, Turbo Prolog encountered the cut. The cut failure caused failure up through the original goal and stopped searching. From this example, we see that Turbo Prolog can backtrack among goals to the left of a cut just as though the cut were not there. By the same token, it can backtrack among goals to the right of the cut so long as the cut is not activated by backtracking. That is, we could write the rule

```
picnic(Day) :- !, weather(Day,fair),
               weekend(Day).
Goal: make(potato_salad,When).
When = saturday
When = sunday
2 solutions
```

In this example, Turbo Prolog succeeded in matching all three of the subgoals in the body of the picnic rule and reported

```
When = saturday
```

Turbo Prolog then backtracked, but only through the two right-most goals. New matches with When instantiated to sunday allowed the goals to succeed so Turbo Prolog reported

```
When = sunday
```

Further processing, however, forces backtracking to the cut. With cut's failure, the parent goal

```
picnic(When).
```

failed and no more matches were considered.

The overall effect of including a cut as a goal is to force Turbo Prolog to limit alternatives. When the cut is activated as a goal, all the choices that have been made since the activation of the parent goal are set. That is, they are treated as if they were the only choice possible. This includes the choice of rules as well as matches and instantiations. Later, when the cut is encountered in backtracking, no other alternatives will be considered for these choices.

EXERCISES 6.3 ▬▬▬▬▬▬▬▬▬▬▬▬▬▬▬▬▬▬▬▬▬▬▬▬▬▬▬▬▬▬▬▬▬▬▬▬▬▬

1. Given this modified database, how will Turbo Prolog answer the query?
   ```
   holiday(tuesday,july_4).
   weather(saturday,fair).
   weekend(saturday).
   weekend(sunday).
   make(potato_salad,Day) :- picnic(Day).
   picnic(Day) :- holiday(Day,july_4), !.
   picnic(Day) :- weather(Day,fair),
                      weekend(Day).
   Goal: make(potato_salad,When).
   ```
2. How will Turbo Prolog respond to the query if the first picnic rule were modified
   ```
   picnic(Day) :- !, holiday(Day,july_4).
   Goal: make(potato_salad,When).
   ```
3. Using the rule from Exercise 2 above, what fact could be added to the database to result in a second day being reported to the same query?

▬▬

6.4 USING CUT

Turbo Prolog programmers use cut to limit the backtracking and attempts at re-satisfying that their programs do. Eliminating unprofitable searches improves Turbo Prolog's efficiency and can make a program more effective. In deciding to use cut, however, the programmer must be aware that these gains may be at the price of the generality of the program.

One specific reason for using cut is to give priority to a specific instantiation of a variable. For example, in the exercises above we saw that the picnic rule with july_4 in it was put first in the multiple picnic rule and the cut was put at its end. Turbo Prolog returned only tuesday.

```
picnic(Day) :- holiday(Day,july_4), !.
picnic(Day) :- weather(Day,fair), weekend(Day).
```

The cut in this database effectively changed the meaning of our query from "when can we have a picnic" to "if it's the Fourth of July, of course we'll have the picnic then; forget anything else."

By the same token, in an earlier example we used

```
picnic(Day) :- weather(Day,fair),weekend(Day),!.
```

This can be used to mean "we're not going to picnic both days this weekend; one's enough."

In a similar manner, we can use cut to limit a search when we know there will only be one right answer.

For example, we might have a class list with student names, social security numbers and some other data. We might write a rule that given a social security number, reports the student's last name. Since social security numbers are unique, there will be no duplicates in a correct database. One match has been made; there is no point in looking for further solutions.

To accomplish this elimination of extra searching, we will put a cut at the end of the rule.

```
id(Lname,SSnumber) :-
                   person(Lname,_,SSnumber,_,_,_),!.
```

When the goal in the first part of the rule has been satisfied, the cut will succeed and one solution will be reported. Backtracking for further search will immediately encounter the cut and the goal in the head of the rule will fail. Further useless searching will not be carried out.

Similarly, adding a cut at the end of the rule is one way to correct the problem we had in Section 5.6 with the reverse rule. When we gave Turbo Prolog a goal of the form

```
reverse(List,[a,b]).
```

the backtracking created uncontrolled processing. We know, however, that a list can have only one "reverse" so looking for other solutions is pointless. If we add a cut to the recursive rule, it will work properly whichever argument is instantiated.

```
reverse([ ],[ ]).
reverse([Head|Tail],List) :-
                    reverse(Tail,Result),
                    append(Result,[Head],List),!.
```

The cut is appropriate and useful in these circumstances:

- when there are several parts of a multiple rule that define different criteria for the same conclusion of which only one should be chosen
- when it is known that there will only be one correct answer and further matching attempts are futile.

Both of these uses require that the programmer take a specific view of the role of the program. Adding the cut narrows down the generality of the program segment. For example,

```
grandfather(Oldster,Kid) :-
        father(Adult,Kid), !, father(Oldster,Adult).
```

Adding the cut to the rule improves efficiency for searches looking for a grand-father when the Kid is known. The cut forces the end of a search if the Kid's father is found but the father of the father cannot be found. The rule is effective because individuals (typically) have only one father and there is no sense searching for another.

Fathers, however, often do have more than one child. This rule would not work correctly if the instantiations are going from father to child. Thus the rule can be used effectively to find the grandfather, but not to find the grandchildren.

To see how this works, consider the database and the examples below. The three examples show the rule working (1) correctly, (2) correctly and efficiently, (3) incorrectly because of the particular query.

```
father(garth,lou).
father(garth,sam).
father(sam,tom).
father(sam,joe).
grandfather(Oldster,Kid) :-
        father(Adult,Kid), !, father(Oldster,Adult).

Goal: grandfather(Old,tom).
        first activate father(Adult,tom).
                succeeds with Adult: sam
        then activate cut, succeeds
        then activate father(Oldster,sam).
                succeeds with Oldster: garth

Goal: grandfather(Old,lou).
        first activate father(Adult,lou).
                succeeds with Adult: garth
        then activate cut, succeeds
        then activate father(Oldster,garth).
                fails, backtrack over cut
        fail grandfather(Oldster,lou).
```

Note: the search for another match to father(Adult,lou) was not done as it was pointless.

```
Goal: grandfather(garth,Kid).
        first activate father(Adult,Kid).
                succeeds with Adult: garth and Kid: lou
        then activate cut, succeeds
        then activate father(garth,garth).
                fails, backtrack over the cut
                fail grandfather(garth,Kid).
```

Note: further search would have found matches but the cut prevented them. By the same token, our earlier rule with names and social security numbers would not find more than one person who had the same last name.

Whenever a programmer uses rules that contain cut, he or she should exercise care that the rules will only be asked to carry out the task for which they were designed.

Cut/Fail Combination

Another use of the cut is in combination with a predicate, fail. The fail predicate is built into the Turbo Prolog system and when activated as a goal, immediately fails. Thus, it always causes backtracking.

The cut/fail combination is used where there are some instantiations of a predicate that should be eliminated from consideration by a rule. Usually the rule will be a multiple rule that handles a number of different criteria; the expression of the multiple rule can be simplified greatly by eliminating some cases at first. Here is an example based on requirements for having a pet in an apartment building.

```
allow(elephant) :- !,fail.
allow(Animal) :- size(Animal,less_than_50_lb),
                 license(Animal).
allow(Animal) :- lives(Animal,cage).
```

The purpose of the first rule in the multiple definition of allow in this example is to remove consideration of elephants at the very start. Because of the cut/fail combination, none of the other allow rules will be checked for matching. This provision eliminates even very small elephants that live in cages. It says no elephants need be proposed. A request for elephants may well have failed eventually in the case, perhaps when licensing requirements could not be met, but the cut/fail combination yields the "no solution" promptly.

Negation

The cut/fail combination is one way to use negation in a Turbo Prolog base. The example above could be paraphrased to

1. If the animal is not an elephant, weighs less than fifty pounds and has a license, it is allowed.
2. If the animal is not an elephant, and lives in a cage, it is allowed.

This use of negation has a powerful effect because the special elephant case need only be entered once, yet it affects use of any of the allow rules. This power has a price: these rules will not work to generate all possible allowed animals; it will only check particular animals.

```
Goal: allow(What).
No solution
```

Again, the programmer must be alert to the intended use of a program and if the use changes, all uses of cut must be reconsidered.

Another method of introducing negation to a Turbo Prolog program is through a special built-in predicate, not. This negation is quite different in that it can be applied selectively to specific rules. It is important to notice that this negation is also based on a different mechanism. For the goal of

```
not(some_goal).
```

to succeed, the goal, some_goal, must fail in a search through the database.

For example, consider this clauses section.

```
clauses
    order(Vegetable) :- not(green(Vegetable)).
    green(beans).
    green(broccoli).
    green(spinach).
    Goal: order(spinach).
    False
```

This answered correctly as spinach, being green, should not be ordered.

```
Goal: order(cauliflower).
True
```

This answered correctly as cauliflower, not being green, should be ordered.

```
Goal: order(collard_greens).
True
```

This is not correct from our view; collard greens are green. The problem is that Turbo Prolog did not have a fact that says collard greens are green, so by the closed world assumption, they could not be. By the same token, a query with a variable will not work. The variable will be instantiated in the first match it makes, causing the match to succeed and the not to fail. This will be the case even if references to other vegetables appear further in the database. In a Turbo Prolog program not(some_goal) is true if some_goal fails within the base.

Rules of Thumb for Cut

The purpose in using cut in a Turbo Prolog program is to modify the processing pattern. As we have discussed, the cut can be used to give some conditions priority over others and to save some time and work on Turbo Prolog's part. These uses of the cut typically limit a query to checking facts rather than generating possible variable instantiations.

Cut is also used to make a recursive rule workable that, when generating variable instantiations, would go on infinitely. The cut is not used in this manner to "fix" an uncontrolled recursion. Rather, there are certain problems whose solutions require generation of an unknown number of possibilities before the desired choice is found. For example, you may be searching through a class roster, looking for a student who earned 100% on an exam. As soon as you find one, you will stop looking. For this kind of problem, the Turbo Prolog program may use the cut as a stopping condition.

Using cut sometimes makes a Turbo Prolog program harder to read and understand. A cut construct can often be eliminated by using not instead, which makes the program easier to read. In other cases, however, the cut is necessary for controlling processing.

EXERCISES 6.4

1. If not were not a built-in predicate, an equivalent could be written using cut/fail. Write a rule in place of

    order(Vegetable).

    from above that replaces the not. It will require two rules.

2. Assume you have added the predicate and a number of facts that note vegetables that are yellow. For example

    yellow(squash).

    a) Write a new rule for

       order(Vegetable)

       that says to order a vegetable that is neither green nor yellow.
    b) Write a new (multiple) rule for

       order(Vegetable)

       that says to order a vegetable if it is not green or if it is not yellow.
    c) What must be true of a vegetable to make Turbo Prolog respond "False" to an order query based on the rule in part (b)?

6.5 PROGRAM OPTIMIZATIONS

The Turbo Prolog system has a number of facilities built into it that are designed to increase the speed and space efficiency of programs. Turbo Prolog programs are compiled for faster operation. Compilation is a translation process that changes the program from the form in which it was written to a form that the underlying machine can process more readily.

The compilation process (which is done automatically when you key in "r" for run) allows Turbo Prolog to analyze your program and organize the representation of facts and rules in a way that speeds up the search and pattern matching. The declaration of object types that we have seen in the domains sections and as arguments in the predicates sections facilitates this organization. For example, if an argument is a symbol rather than an integer, Turbo Prolog will not have to be prepared to do arithmetic with it. Also, the typing of compound objects tells the system the form of the object so components of it can be accessed. Specification of types is important to Turbo Prolog. We will see in Chapter 10 that there are additional important purposes for the typing facility in Turbo Prolog.

During the compilation process, Turbo Prolog is able to optimize some parts of your program. Specifically, tail recursion (a recursive rule where the recurrence of the predicate from the head appears at the right end of the rule) is translated into a simple repetition structure which is more space and time efficient.

Another way to make repeating processes more space and time efficient is to use backtracking instead of recursion when a sequence of subgoals should be cycled through. Forcing backtracking is accomplished through the use of a system-provided predicate, fail, which is a goal that always fails. If you put the fail at the end of a sequence of goals and a predicate at the beginning that always succeeds, the sequence of goals will be repeatedly processed. The predicate name usually used in this mechanism is repeat. Repeat is defined as

```
repeat.
repeat :- repeat.
```

This predicate always succeeds but in the meanwhile it takes the Turbo Prolog out of the scope of the original sequence of goals, so all variables are uninstantiated. Because the sequence of goals has unlimited restarts provided by the repeat, some other mechanism must be used to terminate the processing of the rule. There are complete examples of using this mechanism in Chapters 7 and 8.

There are frequently ways to rewrite rules that are more efficient. For example, the reverse rule that we used in Chapter 5 required the support of the append rule. Another way of writing reverse has fewer rules, but more arguments.

```
new_rev(List,[],List).
new_rev(L1,[H|Tail2],L2) :-
                new_rev([H|L1],Tail2,L2).
```

This rule is more efficient but there are tradeoffs. It is hard to read and understand than the rule for reverse used in Chapter 5. Also, it will only work with one pattern of arguments: the first list must be instantiated and the second uninstantiated when it is used. Modifications made for the sake of space and time efficiency usually result in loss of flexibility.

SUMMARY

Any Turbo Prolog program can be considered descriptively (as a definition) and also prescriptively (as a procedure). The programmer must consider pragmatic matters in the Turbo Prolog system as well as the logical correctness of the program.

The programmer exerts control over processing by arranging rules and facts in a particular order or by using special predicates, particularly cut, to control the Turbo Prolog search pattern.

Descriptive Semantics	Prescriptive Semantics
Declarative	Procedural
Definitions	Directions
Logic	Control
Completeness/correctness	Efficiency
Analysis of problem	Process of solution
World-definition	Set of directions
What is done	How it is done

EXERCISES CHAPTER 6 ━━━━━━━━━━━━━━━

1. Identify the Turbo Prolog concept or concepts described by each phrase below.
   a) Two ways to view a Turbo Prolog program.
   b) These can be satisfied and re-satisfied.
   c) Two concerns that we can consider separately when writing a Turbo Prolog program.
   d) Stepping back to a decision point to make a new choice.
   e) A built-in predicate that cuts off alternative choices.
   f) The group of rules that share the same predicate in their head.
   g) In the descriptive view of Turbo Prolog, the way facts and rules are treated.
   h) In the prescriptive view of Turbo Prolog, the way facts and rules are treated.

2. Using the Turbo Prolog database given below, diagram the goals/subgoals and the processing path for the question.

```
flower(roses,red).
flower(violets,blue).
clothes(hat,blue).
clothes(coat,white).
Goal: flowers(What,Color),
      clothes(Which,Color).
```

3. a) Given this database and query, Turbo Prolog responds "no solution." Explain the processing that results in this response.

```
allow(elephant) :- !, fail.
allow(Animal) :- lives(Animal,cage).
lives(boa,cage).
Goal: allow(What).
```

b) If the database were rearranged, how and why would the question be answered now?

```
allow(Animal) :- lives(Animal,cage).
allow(elephant) :- !, fail.
lives(boa,cage).
Goal: allow(What).
```

4. Write a Turbo Prolog program of rules for a diet, specifying food items that are acceptable for eating. Include rules for at least three items that are not acceptable, and put rules to exclude them first in the database.

7

Using Built-in Predicates

The purpose of this chapter is to help the learner:

■ be aware of many of the predicates that are available in Turbo Prolog.
■ understand a conceptual grouping of built-in predicates for
   facilitating reference.
   understanding roles.

7.1 ROLES OF BUILT-IN PREDICATES

As part of the Turbo Prolog system, certain capabilities are provided. A few of these capabilities are part of the system structure. For example, the prompts (Goal:) and the organization of the database are designed into the software that is in control of the programming environment. These capabilities are necessary so that we can actually use the language in conjunction with a computer system.

Other capabilities are made available to the programmer through built-in predicates. These predicates are used just like the predicates that you as the programmer design. They are, however, available for use without the need for defining them in the predicates section of the program. The programmer can use these predicates in the body of rules or in goals entered through a dialog query.

While some of the built-in predicates are simply for convenience, most of them are needed because they do tasks that are not possible in the pure declarative model. Input and output control are examples of these kinds of predicates. A program, being a set of facts and rules of which questions are asked, has no place for interaction with a universe outside the world that the program's database defines. Any action on the part of the Turbo Prolog program that goes beyond pattern-matching and variable instantiation is outside the pure declarative model. These actions are called *side-effects* of the predicates.

When we define predicates in the predicates section, we have to specify the type of each of the arguments in the predicate. By the same token, built-in predicates also have a specific number of arguments and a predetermined type to go with each argument. In addition to the simple symbol types we have used and the structured types such as lists, there are several others: integer and real for numbers (Chapter 9), file for storage (Chapter 8) and char and string which are discussed in this chapter, section 2.

Besides the specification of the type for each argument, built-in predicates have *flow patterns*. When a predicate that includes variables is activated as a goal, the variables may or may not be instantiated to a constant value. The flow pattern defines which must be instantiated (those that could be making information flow into the goal) and those that must be uninstantiated (available for information to flow out of the goal). We will see that some built-in predicates have only one acceptable flow pattern while others have several flow patterns so that they may be used in several ways.

The predicates built-in to the Turbo Prolog system can be grouped according to the kind of task they are designed to do. These roles include

- input and output,
- interacting with the system,
- modification of processing pattern (control),
- doing arithmetic,
- building and manipulating data objects,
- building and modifying databases.

In addition to providing information on specific predicates, this chapter is designed to provide the reader with some structure within which to organize the predicates. Input and output, modification of processing, doing arithmetic and interacting with the system are all discussed in greater detail in other chapters in this book. They are included here because this chapter addresses the grouping of predicates. Understanding this organization of predicates makes it easier to choose the appropriate predicates for the task at hand.

Input and Output

In the declarative model, the database is the description of a world. To explore the world or derive information from it, we ask questions and receive answers. The question and answer communication is our interaction with Turbo Prolog. Unless we specify some other source and receiver for the questioning/answering, the interaction is with the user. In cases where we want to modify the standard question/answer dialog, we need to use predicates that handle input and output.

Many of the input and output predicates allow us to modify the form of the interaction. The basic dialog interaction is terse and assumes the user needs no information beyond the standard prompt, Goal: and the assertion-based answers.

Usually we would prefer a different form of the interaction that makes it easier for a person to use the program. When the user wants to give input to the program but is constrained by syntax specifications to a rigid and unnatural formulation, the user's task is more difficult. The programmer can develop input procedures that allow more natural forms of input or at least explain the required form when there is one.

Similarly, when there is output data to be given to the user, some explanation is often helpful. Also, output frequently consists of much more than just data. With Turbo Prolog we have facility to produce graphic and sound output as well as text. More detail and examples of the input/output predicates appear in Chapter 8. One of the major goals in the Turbo Prolog design is the creation of directly executable, user-oriented programs. In this kind of programming, input and output are very important.

Interacting with the System

Interaction between the active program and other parts of the Turbo Prolog system is related to the input/output considerations and is also discussed further in Chapter 8. The Turbo Prolog system allows a program to access the editing and file management facility that is part of the larger environment. The ability to use these system components gives the programmer access to the editor and file manager as prewritten tools.

The second reason for interacting with the system is to allow the source of questions or receiver of answers to be a file rather than the user. A file is a more appropriate source when the question that is to be processed is long or complex (for example, a paragraph to be searched for spelling errors). A file is also a good choice for results that we need to retain after the Turbo Prolog interaction is over.

Processing Control

Some special symbols we have been using since the beginning of the book communicate to Turbo Prolog about processing. The comma in conjunctions and the period at the end of clauses give specific signals as part of the control mechanism. Similarly, not and the cut, !, which are discussed in Chapter 6, modify the standard control process.

A pair of built-in predicates that can affect the processing pattern are **free** and **bound**. These predicates are written with a single variable name as an argument.

free(X) will succeed if X is uninstantiated
bound(X) will succeed if X is instantiated

They can be used as guards for predicates that have specific requirements for flow patterns, either because they are built-in predicates or because they have been defined by the programmer. For example, in Chapter 6 we saw a rule for grandfather that included a cut to make it more efficient while limiting its usefulness to queries where the grandchild is known and the grandfather sought.
We could guard the rule with either free or **bound**.

```
grandfather(Oldster,Kid) :- bound(Kid),
                            father(Adult,Kid), !,
                            father(Oldster,Adult).
```

We could follow this rule with other grandfather rules that would be used in cases where the bound goal's failure prevented use of this rule.

In a dialog, when we specify a goal that has more than one solution, the system automatically backtracks to seek all solutions. Sometimes we do not want this automatic backtracking. As we have seen, we can alter the standard behavior with the cut, but there is another mechanism that limits the search to one solution. This is to put the goal in the program rather than entering it as part of the dialog. The goal has its own program section and keyword, goal.

```
goal
    order(Vegetable).
```

This goal is internal to the program in contrast to the external goals asked in the dialog. The goal section must be placed after the predicates section of the program if it uses predicates defined in the program. It can come before or after the clauses section. There can only be one goal internal to the program. An internal goal also behaves differently in that none of the instantiations are reported. Rather, all sub-goals are carried out until the main goal is satisfied, then the user is asked to press the space bar to go back to the environment menu. All program communication with the user must be through input/output predicates.

Thus it is more likely that you as a programmer will want to use an internal goal for reasons other than to control the number of solutions. In fact it is more likely you will want the opposite: to use an internal goal for its self-starting behavior and yet be able to get multiple solutions. You can accomplish the repeated searches by writing a recursive goal or by using fail.

Fail is a predicate that can be used in other roles in several mechanisms that modify processing. Since fail always fails when it is activated as a goal, it always causes backtracking. That means that if we have a predicate that we want to reactivate, we can follow it by fail. Say we wanted an internal goal to write all the values for an argument in a set of facts in our database about the week's weather, a goal that would accomplish it is

```
Goal: weather(Day,Outlook), write(Outlook), fail.
```

Each time weather succeeds, write will succeed, doing output of the value, then fail will cause backtracking. Write, being an input/output predicate, cannot be resatisfied, so backtracking goes to weather. Weather can be resatisfied, so the process starts again. It will repeat until the weather finally exhausts all possibilities, whereupon the goal fails. In the meanwhile, however, all the values for Outlook have been printed.

A closely related form allows output for variable values when a predicate has been defined that does not have variables in its head. Normally, an external goal only reports values for variables specified in the query (those that appear in the head of the rules) so any instantiations done for other variables will not be reported. Thus a predicate could be defined:

```
go :- find(Value), write(Value), fail.
```

Again, all the values that make find succeed will be output, while all the user has to do to activate the goal is key in "go" in the dialog.

The fail predicate can also be used in a structure that uses backtracking instead of recursion to repeat processing of a series of goals. In the program, a predicate is defined that will always succeed.

```
repeat.
repeat :- repeat.
```

The repeat is then used as the first goal in a series to be processed.

The repeat predicate, when first encountered in processing, simply succeeds. When backtracking returns to the repeat predicate, processing begins again, just as it did at the first success of the repeat goal. The repeat will continue generalizing new cycles through the process as long as it is backtracked to. To stop the repetition process, backtracking must be stopped. That means that the special case for stopping will succeed instead of fail. For example, this rule reads terms from the user until the word "stop" is reached. Because the repeat predicate takes processing out of the scope of eat words, all old instantiations are discarded, saving space inside the machine:

```
eat_words :- repeat, readln(Item), check(Item), !.
check(stop).
check(Value) :- fail.
```

In the fundamental Turbo Prolog model, recursion provides the facility for causing repetition. The repeat/fail uses a different underlying plan. Recursion can be viewed as the jointed telescope from Chapter 5, where important work is being done both on the way into the problem (left-to-right) and on the way out (right-to-left). The repetition of repeat/fail is more like stroking a cat; the useful work is only one way.

A final use of fail is in the cut/fail combination that we saw in Chapter 6. This combination provides a way of giving particular solutions more importance than others. It can be used to skip some processing in certain cases or to provide a form of negation. Because fail causes backtracking and cut cannot be backtracked over, encountering the cut/fail causes immediate failure of the goal that has called these goals.

```
go_to_work :- day(saturday), !, fail.
```

Another built-in predicate that modifies processing is **exit**. When this goal is activated, the program processing stops and Turbo Prolog returns to the top-level environment screen (from an internal goal) or to the dialog level. Exit can be used for a graceful completion of a program as well as for an emergency escape when some specific (anticipated) error condition arises.

Arithmetic Manipulations

Understanding the built-in predicates for doing arithmetic requires a clear understanding of the difference between an arithmetic expression and an arithmetic value. An arithmetic expression is a sequence of one or more symbols that represent arithmetic operators or arithmetic values. For example:

$$X + Y$$
$$2 + 3$$
$$X - 4$$

Within expressions, variables can represent other expressions. That is, in the examples, X and Y could be expressions themselves. Expressions have no value unless they are *evaluated* by the use of one of the predicates that specifically causes evaluation. Before an expression can be evaluated, any variables in the expression must be instantiated to numeric values.

The arithmetic operators, like + and −, are predicates, but they do not cause evaluation. The predicates for comparing two expressions do cause evaluation. For example <, which is read "is less than," causes evaluation of the two expressions with it. For example,

$$X + 2 < Y - 1$$

When this goal is activated, X and Y must have values so that the expressions can be evaluated. If, after evaluation, the first expression value is less than the second, this goal will succeed. Such a goal could appear in a rule:

```
correct_pair :- readint(X), readint(Y),
                X + 2 < Y - 1.
```

The syntax of the arithmetic goal looks much different from most goals we have seen. Because most people are more familiar with arithmetic forms like the ones in this example, Turbo Prolog has special facility to allow that form.

The predicate = serves two roles in arithmetic manipulation. It is the comparison that forces evaluation of two expressions and returns "true" if the values are equal. The same operator is used to evaluate an expression and instantiate a variable to that value. For example, the goal

```
Square = X * X.
```

can instantiate Square to the square of X. In this use of =, X must have a value so the expression can be evaluated, but Square need not. If Square has a value, = works as a comparison test; if it does not already have a value, it will be given that value. A more extended discussion of Turbo Prolog's arithmetic capability appears in Chapter 9.

EXERCISES 7.1

1. Programs with a lot of input and output tend to be explained procedurally rather than descriptively. Why?
2. List at least three ways to control the number of times a goal will be activated.

7.2 BUILDING AND MANIPULATING DATA OBJECTS

Several predicates create or modify objects, including changing objects from one type to another. Most of these apply to the standard non-numeric types: symbol, character (written char) and string.

A character in programming is a letter (upper or lower case), a numeral, one of a set of special symbols like punctuation, or one of a set of non-printing characters. These non-printing characters have meaning in a computer system, typically representing some control function. For example, "return" has a non-printing character and so does "back-space."

The internal representation for characters in the computer is as integers. Each character has a unique integer associated with it. A standard has been set up, called the American Standard Code for Information Interchange, so that different computers use the same representation. There is a chart showing the ASCII (pronounced ask-key) code in Appendix A of this book.

A string is a sequence of zero or more characters, handled as a unit. The characters in a string are usually printing characters, either letters, numerals or punctuation marks. However, non-printing characters are useful in controlling the output of strings. The string type and the built-in predicates that go with it provide a simple and powerful way to handle many non-numeric programming problems.

For the symbol type, a constant is written beginning with a lower-case character. For the character type, a constant is written enclosed in single quote marks. For the string type, a constant is written enclosed in double quote marks. Turbo Prolog often converts values from symbol to string type and vice versa for convenience in the dialog.

Strings can be built up, taken apart or modified with programmer-defined rules using built-in predicates. One of the simplest string manipulation predicates is **concat** which defines the concatenation of strings. The predicate has three arguments. When concat is activated as a goal, at least two of the arguments must be instantiated.

```
concat("This","String,"Result).
Result = "ThisString"
1 solution

concat(First,"String","ThisString").
First = "This"
1 solution

concat("This",Second,"ThisString").
Second = "String"
1 solution
```

Another simple string manipulation predicate is str_len which has two arguments, a string and its length. When a str_len goal is activated, the string must be instantiated but the length may or may not. The length argument will be of integer type. As with other string predicates, a variable may be instantiated to an empty string.

```
Goal: str_len("",L).
L = 0
1 solution
```

Turbo Prolog also provides a predicate that identifies a string that meets the specification for a legal variable or constant name. That predicate, isname, requires that the string that is its only argument be instantiated. As a goal, isname can be used as a guard in a rule the same way as bound and free were used earlier.

A predicate that disassembles a string is frontstr. This predicate requires two instantiated arguments, an integer and a string, and two uninstantiated arguments, strings that will allow outflow of the disassembled string. The number of characters indicated by the integer will be taken from the front of the given string and instantiated as a string to the third argument; the leftover will be instantiated to the fourth argument. If the integer value is larger than the length of the instantiated string, the predicate will fail.

Say for example you have a class list of students' social security numbers (nine numerals) but you want to use only the last four numerals as an identification number.

```
predicates
    student_id(string,symbol)
    student_ss(string,symbol)
clauses
    student_id(Short_form,Name) :-
            student_ss(Long_form,Name),
            frontstr(5,Long_form,_,Short_form).
```

Two other string predicates that can be used to disassemble or assemble strings are frontchar and fronttoken. These two predicates are very similar to the append rules we defined for lists in Chapter 5, except that in frontchar and fronttoken the major string is the first argument and the second and third arguments are the components. In frontchar, the second argument will be a single character. In fronttoken, the second argument will be a token, a sequence of characters that could be a meaningful part of a Turbo Prolog program. Such a sequence might be a name (e.g., a constant or a number) or a character (e.g., a question mark). Fronttoken uses blanks as dividers and ignores them if there are extras. The blanks are used as empty space rather than meaningful characters.

Here is a program that marks the magic words in a string by changing them to upper case. It uses another built-in predicate, upper_lower, which is defined for strings but can be used on names because Turbo Prolog coerces the symbols into strings and back. Since blanks are removed by fronttoken, they are individually replaced in the modified string by using frontchar.

```
predicates
   magic(symbol,symbol)
   changer(string,string)
clauses
   magic(Old,New) :- upper_str_len(Old,4),
                        lower(New,Old).
   magic(Old,Old).
   changer("","").
   changer(Plain,Marked) :-
           fronttoken(Plain,Word,Remains),
           magic(Word,New_word),
           changer(Remains,New_remainder),
           fronttoken(Middle,New_word,New_remainder),
           frontchar(Marked,' ',Middle), !.
Goal: changer("How is this",New).
New = How is THIS
```

The second changer rule includes a cut to prevent attempts at resatisfying the rule. Having more than one choice for the magic rule allows for a second way of returning a new (the old) string from changer, so the backtracking could also have been controlled by including a cut at the end of the first part of the magic rule.

The changer rule requires that the first argument be instantiated and the second be uninstantiated. While using a cut can have this effect, in the changer rule it is a result of the flow pattern of fronttoken, which must have at least some arguments instantiated.

An additional set of predicates allows conversion of values from one data type to another.

Predicate	Converts Between	
str_int	string	integer
str_real	string	real
str_char	string	char
char_int	char	its ASCII integer equivalent

Turbo Prolog also includes a set of special predicates that are called comparison operators. They are discussed more extensively in Chapter 9 because they are commonly used in numeric problems to determine whether two numbers are equal or whether one is greater than the other.

These comparison operators can, however, be used on any of the standard domain types we have been discussing. Additionally, the operator for equality, =, can be used on lists and other compound structures. Of course, the pattern matching ability that is built into Turbo Prolog is an effective way to test for equality of values, too.

With strings and characters, a value being greater than another value is quite like being further in alphabetical order. The order is actually based on the ASCII order of the characters that make up a string, so including numbers or upper-case characters will affect the ordering.

EXERCISES 7.2

1. Using the database with the changer rule above:
   a) Identify the rule that determines which words are special.
   b) Rewrite the rule so that every word starting with 'a' will be capitalized.
   c) Rewrite the rule so that only the words "is" and "did" will be capitalized.
2. In the database above with the rule to find id numbers from social security numbers, what would be the result if the id's were actually instantiated as integers instead of strings?

7.3 MODIFYING THE DATABASE

The creation of a correct, complete database is the central task for the programmer. The database contains the definitions of all rules and facts, all the assertions from which information can be derived. The database describes a closed world which Turbo Prolog assumes is complete and consistent. While it is the world that is described, it is the database that the programmer actually enters into the computer.

In all the programs we have seen so far, the complete database was developed and entered into the computer through a program file built in the editor. It is also possible to enter new facts and delete existing facts in the database while the program is being executed, either by activating goals in programmer-defined rules or through the dialog. While entering new facts into the database may not make sense, given the closed world assumption, it is often a good approach to solving some kinds of programming problems, especially those that are complex or not clearly understood. As the problem becomes better understood or special cases are isolated, the database can be modified to meet the new requirements.

The built-in predicates used to modify a database are asserta and assertz (or optionally assert), which add facts to the database, at the top and the bottom, respectively, of the set of facts of the same form, and retract, which removes a specified fact from the database. Retract can be used with a variable and back-tracking to delete all facts of the specified form or controlled with cut to eliminate only the first instance of the specified form.

If we are going to be introducing new facts into our database during the execution of the program we have to give Turbo Prolog forewarning and specify the structure of the new facts. We do this through a special section in our program identified by the keyword database. The database section precedes the predicates section but follows the domains section if there is one.

The following example has a rule that asserts facts as well as having a fact of the specified form already in the database.

```
database
    recorded(symbol)
predicates
    remember(symbol)
clauses
    remember(Place) :- asserta(recorded(Place)).
    recorded(home).
Goal: recorded(What).
What = home
1 solution
Goal: remember(vacation).
True
Goal: recorded(What).
What = vacation
What = home
2 solutions
```

We might expand this program by developing a rule that reports the argument of a fact, then moves the fact to the bottom of the sequence of facts in the database. The rule will have a cut to prevent backtracking.

```
suggest(Memory) :- retract(recorded(Memory)),
                   assertz(recorded(Memory)), !.
```

Facts that are asserted or retracted using the database mechanism remain in effect until the program is recompiled, usually when a change has been made in the program using the editor or when the program is stored on disk and then later retrieved for use. If you have used the database mechanism to modify the facts that are in a program, you may want to be able to use the up-dated database at a later time. The built-in predicate save allows you to retain the current database of the facts that were specified as database facts, saved in a disk file under the name you give as an argument to save. All facts that are part of the database form are saved whether they were entered as part of the original program or were entered during a run. The facts that have been saved in the file are retrieved and replaced in the active database by the use of the predicate consult which takes a file name for its argument.

A final predicate that does not so much alter the database as to analyze it is findall. Findall searches through the database and gathers instances of objects into a list. To use findall we specify a goal and a variable in the goal. The predicate searches through the database to find all appearances of the goal that can be proved true. For each true goal, the constant value that was instantiated to the specified variable is gathered in to a list. The list is instantiated to the variable given in the third argument of the predicate. If there are no occurrences, the goal returns an empty list.

The third argument of findall is a list, so anytime you want to use this predicate you must specify a domain type of a list made up of the type of object that findall will find. Having defined the list in the domain, you may use findall freely, including using it through the dialog while a program is executing.

The database below shows several ways of using the findall predicate.

```
domains
    list = symbol*
predicates
    parent(symbol,symbol)
    rule1(list)
    rule2(list,symbol)
    rule3(list,symbol)
clauses
    parent(jan,bet).
    parent(jan,cat).
    parent(joe,ann).
    parent(joe,cat).
    rule1(Collection) :-
                    findall(C,parent(_,C),Collection).
    rule2(Collection,P) :-
                    findall(C,parent(P,C),Collection).
    rule3(Collection,P) :- parent(P,_),
                    findall(C,parent(P,C),Collection).
```

The use of findall in rule1 is the most general form. The predicate collects all the constant values that appear as the second argument in the parent predicate. The values are entered into a list with any duplicate values retained.

```
Goal: rule1(List).
List = [bet,cat,ann,cat]
1 solution
```

The second rule, rule2, allows us to limit the values gathered by specifying a constant for the first argument of the parent predicate.

```
Goal: rule2(List,jan).
List = [bet,cat]
1 solution
```

If findall is given a value for the first argument that does not appear in the database, an empty list will be created.

```
Goal: rule2(List,sam).
List = [ ]
1 solution
```

However, if we use this rule without specifying the constant in the activation, findall will gather all the instances of the second argument into the list and report the last value for the first argument as the solution.

```
Goal: rule2(List,P)
List = [bet,cat,ann,cat], P = joe
1 solution
```

Rule3 is more effective for separating out the constants that go with each instance of the value of the first argument. A list is generated for each of the parent facts.

```
Goal: rule3(List,P).
List = [bet,cat], P = jan
List = [bet,cat], P = jan
List = [ann,cat], P = joe
List = [ann,cat], P = joe
4 solutions
```

Findall puts an unusual constraint on the variable used to indicate which values are gathered. The scope of this variable is limited to the predicate itself. Thus the variable cannot be instantiated before findall is called and it is no longer instantiated after the predicate is finished. The list variable and others in the clause have their normal scope, instantiated until the end of the clause's activation. The list does not continue to exist after the end of the clause, however. Even though findall builds the list, the programmer must keep track of it (perhaps using asserta) if it is to be needed later.

EXERCISES 7.3

1. Assuming facts about a week's weather of the form

   ```
   weather(<day>,<outlook>).
   ```

   write a rule that lists all seven of the days' outlooks.

2. Using the same form of facts as above, write a rule that will gather a list of days with similar outlook on the weather.

3. Write a rule that retracts a fact of the form

   ```
   idea(<object>)
   ```

   adds an 'x' to the front of the object name, then asserts the fact in the new form.

SUMMARY

A large number of predicates are built-in to Turbo Prolog so that the programmer may use them without having to define them. Built-in predicates in some cases are just for the programmers convenience. In other cases, they handle tasks, such as input and output, that are outside the pure declarative model of success of goals within a defined database. Associated with each predicate is a flow pattern that specifies which argument must be or must not be instantiated when the predicate is activated.

Built-in predicates fall into categories according to the roles they serve. Those roles are:

- input and output,
- interacting with the system,
- modification of processing pattern (control),
- doing arithmetic,
- building and manipulating data objects,
- building and modifying databases.

The programmer who understands the task to be done can use this organization to look for the appropriate predicate to facilitate programming that task.

EXERCISES CHAPTER 7

1. In this chapter, six roles of built-in predicates are listed. For each role, specify a programming problem that will require using a built-in predicate from that group.

2. Write Turbo Prolog programs for these problems.

a) Go through a database of facts of the form

   ```
   made_of(<fruit>,<product>).
   ```

   to find all the products made of each fruit.

b) Write a rule to remove duplicate entries from a list of constants.

c) Write a rule to alphabetize a list of values.

d) Use the database from above to find an alphabetized list of products for each fruit.

e) Use the same database to find an alphabetized list of products for all fruit together.

8

Input, Output and the Environment

The purpose of this chapter is to help the learner:

- read and write using various input/output streams.
- do screen input/output.
- consider some facets of building a user interface.
- understand the general workings of the programming environment.

8.1 INPUT AND OUTPUT STREAMS

Input, the data that a program receives while it is running, and output, the data that the program reports to the user, are important parts of the dynamic behavior of a program. While we may have programs that do not require any input, programs that do not output any results are not very useful. We speak of reading the input and writing the output even though we may not actually be handling data that could be written (e.g., writing an end-of-line marker).

As a generalization in computing, a source of items for a computer to process is called the *input stream* and the place where results of the processing are going is called the *output stream*. In Turbo Prolog the keyboard is the default input stream and the screen is the default output stream. (*Default* simply means the choice a computer system will make if it has not been given any other directions.) The screen and keyboard are predefined input/output devices.

Other sources and receivers of data can be used by a program. There are two predefined devices that can receive output: the printer and the communication port. The screen can be read from, as well as written to, through the use of special screen-handling predicates. Files are also used for input and output, but rather than being predefined, they must be defined individually. The *file domain* is used to define particular files for program processing.

For some kinds of programming tasks, files have advantages over the keyboard and screen for input and output. There may be a great number of items that need to be processed the same way, or the data to be processed may be preprocessed and on a disk file. For output, it may be helpful to have a record of the answers or results of the process for use later. The Turbo Prolog system has mechanisms, again built-in predicates, to allow use of specified files for either the input or output stream.

Program processing that works with files and does repeated processing on a large number of data is called *batch* processing, in contrast to *interactive* processing, where the user interacts with the program and the keyboard and screen are typical input and output streams.

File Handling

Two steps are required to use a file for processing. First the file must be specified in the domains section, giving it an internal name called the symbolic name. This is the name by which the program will address the file. The second step is to open the file, associating it with a file name that is the external name, a system DOS file name. Files can be opened in any one of four modes: read, write, append to, or modify. Once a file is opened, it is available to become the current read device or the current write device, depending on which mode it was opened in. Several files may be open at the same time, but each one must have a unique symbolic name. When a file has been designated as the current stream (using readdevice or writedevice and the symbolic name), it can be read from or written to using the usual reading and writing predicates. An additional reading predicate, file_str, reads a complete file from its disk storage directly into a string. Existing files have an *end-of-file* marker that controls the end of the file_str input or can be tested for directly. When the program is finished with its file processing, all files should be closed, using the predicate closefile. An end-of-file mark is placed in the file when it is closed.

Files may also be written and read in programs that use the database domain to create changes in facts during the execution of a program. When database clauses have been generated or modified through asserta, assertz or retract, the changes can be saved in a file by using save. The file can be read and the facts entered into the database through consult. A file created through save can be edited using the system editor like any other file, and can, in fact, be created through the editor and then consulted. Care must be taken in editing such a file, however, because the format of the facts in the file must be precise. The following is an example of creating a file, then reading from the same file and showing the contents of the file on the screen. In writing the value to the file, a string that contains the end-of-line code must be included. This is one of several string command codes that begin with a \.

```
domains
    file = only_one
goal
    write("Type an integer    "),
    readint(Value),
    openwrite(only_one,"one.dat"),
    writedevice(only_one),
    write(Value,"\n"),
    closefile(only_one),
    openread(only_one,"one.dat"),
    readdevice(only_one),
    readint(Again),
    writedevice(screen),
    write(Again),
    closefile(only_one).
```

EXERCISES 8.1

1. In the example above, how many output streams are open when the line

   ```
   write(Again)
   ```

   is executed?
2. a) If instead of writing a single value, we wanted to write several values on one line in the output file, which line would be changed?
   b) If we wanted several values each on its own line, how would we have to modify the program?

8.2 INTERACTIVE INPUT AND OUTPUT

Interactive input and output are usually keyboard and screen based. Input from the keyboard can be controlled on a key-by-key basis or dealt with as strings of various length. The program can also read strings from the screen. Screen output can be presented in different modes: text mode (single screen or through windows) and graphics mode (high or medium resolution).

Keyboard input makes use of the same set of predicates that are used for reading from any input stream.

Predicate	Argument	Behavior
readint	integer	waits, uses carriage-return for end
readln	string	waits, uses carriage-return for end
readreal	real	waits, uses carriage-return for end
readchar	char	waits, gets single character, no carriage-return
inkey	char	does not wait, gets single character, fails if none

Output to the screen in text mode makes use of the very flexible predicate, write, which is able to handle a varying number and varying types of arguments. Additionally, Turbo Prolog has the facility to define *windows*, portions of the screen where different output components can be placed. Defining a number of windows to act as "mini-screens" is like setting up a number of pieces of paper to make notes on different topics, then arraying the pieces of paper on top of a desk. Depending on their size and location, several of them may be visible but the one on top, the current one, is the one available for working with. To get at the next one down, the current one must be removed.

Windows can be set up with different colors, borders, sizes and locations. The predicate to set up windows, makewindow, has eight arguments:

an integer that is the window's reference number
an integer that controls the color and form of the window interior
an integer that controls the color and form of the window border
a string that is the label in the window border
an integer that specifies the row of the upper-left corner (0-24)
an integer that specifies the column of that corner (0-79)
an integer that specifies the number of rows (1-25) including border
an integer that specifies the number of columns (1-80) including border

Note that the color and some other attributes will depend on the particular hardware you are using.

In the example below, two windows are defined and messages are written in each of them sequentially. After each message is written, a pause is provided by asking the program user to key in a character. This character is not used for any purpose; it is the pause waiting for the input that is desired.

```
goal
    makewindow(1,25,32,"one",0,0,25,80),
    write("This is 1"),
    readchar(_),
    makewindow(2,42,32,"two",10,20,10,20),
    write("This is 2"),
    readchar(_),
    shiftwindow(1), nl,
    write("This is 1 again. Press space bar.").
```

In this example, the strings were written in the upper-left corner of the window that was active. The strings could have been placed elsewhere in the window by placing the cursor at the desired location first, using cursor. This predicate takes two arguments, the row and column numbers where the cursor should appear. The numbers are row and column within the window, not within the whole screen, so their value is relative to the window.

In addition to using the usual write predicate, three predicates are used to place text at a location on the screen or to read text that is already at the specified location.

`scr_char(Row,Col,Character)`	for a single character
`field_str(Row,Col,Length,String)`	for a string of characters, length long
`window_str(String)`	for a complete windowful of text

Turbo Prolog also can be used in the graphics mode. In this mode, input and output to the screen is based on single dots instead of character-sized units. Individual dots at specified points or lines between specified points are used to create drawings. Predicates are available to draw directly, to provide an interactive sketch-pad-like drawing system and to add sound to programs.

User Interface

The communication between the computer and the program user is called an *interface*. Developing a good user interface is an important part of writing a program because people's appreciation of a good program depends on how easy it is to use, as much as on how successfully it carries out its central problem solution. The decision about whether to use an internal goal or external goals, for example, has a great effect on the interface the user experiences.

Designing a user interface is a complex task that requires careful thought about the characteristics of the user and the circumstances where the program will be used. The kind of interface that is needed for a novice computer user may not be appropriate for a sophisticated user. Too little communication or display for the user is often a problem, although long and ornate displays of graphic output or too verbose a discussion are equally inappropriate. If a program is being created for someone other than the programmer to use, this is especially important.

In general, the programmer should try to keep the audience in mind, to actually design the user interface instead of just letting it happen, and be prepared to take advice from other people who are willing to try out and constructively criticize the interface. Generally the programmer should plan to test early versions with users to refine the interface for the final version.

EXERCISES 8.2 ━━━━━━━━━━━━━━━━━━━━━━━━━━━━━━━━━

1. Write a program that asks the user what month his or her birthday is and responds either "that's this month!" or "that's a while yet," whichever is appropriate.
2. Using the example in this section, rewrite rules as necessary to make the message start in the middle of each window.

━━

8.3 PROGRAMMING ENVIRONMENT

An environment is something that surrounds us. It affects the way we do things by providing mechanisms for carrying out tasks. A programming environment includes ways to create programs, use programs, store the programs and results, and observe the execution of programs.

In addition to providing an easy-to-use programming environment, Turbo Prolog allows programs to access and use parts of the environment in programs. The main environment is displayed at the top level where the programmer can choose to edit, run, or compile a program, use the filer to handle file storage, or customize the environment.

The editor and the filer are two components of the environment that can be used as part of programs written for particular applications. The editor is available with its full capabilities if it is called with the predicate,

```
edit(Oldstring,Newstring)
```

which allows the currently active window to be used as an edit window. Another predicate, editmsg, allows editing while providing more information to the user.

A related predicate, display, allows the user to look at a string as though it were in the editor, but does not allow the user to make any changes in the string.

File management through the filer is also available in a limited form for use in programs. In section 8.1, we saw how the system file organization is used to access files for input and output. Additionally, the filer can be used through built-in predicates to get directory information, set the default disk drive and check to see if a particular file exists.

A program can use another environment facility, the trace facility. By using trace(on) and trace(off) within a program, partial traces can be shown on the screen. To turn trace on and off, either trace or shorttrace must have been in the original program as a compiler directive.

There are several compiler directives that can be entered at the beginning of the program file to give specific information about how the translation process should be specialized for the specific program. In addition to trace, others like diagnostics, provide data about the structure of the program. Nowarnings suppresses warning about unusual instantiation patterns or free variables, while check_determ adds warnings about nondeterministic rules.

EXERCISES 8.3

1. Adapt the example from section 8.1 to add a trace of the execution of that part of the program where "again" has a value.
2. Write a program that calls the editor when an 'e' is keyed in and ignores any other input.

SUMMARY

Input and output are the communication between the computer and the person using it. Input and output can be batch oriented, in which case files are often used for either or both the input or output streams. Files may also be used in interactive input and output, but more typically, the keyboard is used for the input device and the screen is used for output.

Turbo Prolog has built in facility for a variety of screen modes. Screen communication may be in text mode, which uses the character as the size unit, or in graphics mode, which uses the dot as the size unit. String manipulation predicates are frequently used in input and output, both to actually handle the text and to control placement on the screen or in the file.

Input and output are important in design of the user interface. An easy-to-use and appropriate user interface is an important part of a program. Turbo Prolog makes it possible to access parts of the programming environment from within an executing program so those components can also be used to increase the quality of the program.

EXERCISES CHAPTER 8

1. Each of the following terms is followed by a number of statements. Find ALL of the statements that are true about the terms.
   a) strings
      1) can be written to the screen
      2) may contain screen placement commands
      3) cannot contain numerals
      4) cannot be longer than the window is wide
   b) input stream
      1) may be a file
      2) may be a user
      3) may be source of questions
      4) may be accessed character by character

   c) user interface
      1) requires everything be in same form
      2) requires use of files
      3) requires use of characters
      4) facilitates communication between user and Turbo Prolog

2. Following the three steps below, write a program to build a database of facts of the form

```
made_of(<fruit>),(<products>).
```

  a) Write a user interface requesting the pairs of fruit and product.
  b) Take the pairs the user enters and build facts in the database from them.
  c) When the user indicates the facts are all complete, write the facts out to a file.

3. Write a program that cycles through a pattern of windows with various sizes, locations and screen attributes.

4. Write a program that gets the contents of a text file, lets the user edit it and then writes it to an output file.

9

Doing Arithmetic

The purpose of this chapter is to help the learner:

- understand the mechanism by which Turbo Prolog can be used for
    number manipulation
    number calculation and
    expression evaluation.
- recognize the operators built into the Turbo Prolog system.
- understand operator precedence, position and associativity.

9.1 ARITHMETIC

Number manipulation and calculations can be done within the Turbo Prolog systems. In this chapter, we will look at the *integer* type (which means all numbers are whole numbers) and the *real* type (numbers which may have decimal points and decimal fractions). The range of integers in the Turbo Prolog system is −32768 to 32767. Real numbers have a much larger range with very big or very small real numbers written in scientific notation. In that form, numbers are made of two parts, a base and a power of ten.

Built-in predicates are provided that do arithmetic operations, such as adding, and number comparisons, such as testing for equality. Conceptually, the predicates can be fit into the Turbo Prolog model of defining a predicate, say for multiplication, then having a list of facts to look for a match. This is the same method we use when we learn a "times-table" and remember facts as we need them. Actually, instead of looking them up in a table, computers are finding these values (counting on their fingers as it were) but the effect is the same: the integer arithmetic database is available to use.

Calculation

To do calculation, built-in predicates are used. For example,

```
Sum = 3 + 4.
```

The predicate, =, is an infix operator. An operator is a Turbo Prolog predicate that is specially set up so that it can be used without the normal syntax for predicates, which is

```
<predicate>(<arguments>).
```

Among operators, we can use *infix* which means the operator appears between its arguments, *prefix*, where the operator appears before the arguments, or *postfix*, when the operator appears after the arguments.

```
infix     3 + 4
prefix    + 3 4
postfix   3 4 +
```

Infix, prefix, and postfix are the possible *positions* for operators. Most Turbo Prolog predicates are prefix. In doing arithmetic, however, we use infix because that is the form we are most used to using to do arithmetic.

In the example

```
Sum = 3 + 4.
```

there are two infix operators, = and +. The = instantiates a variable while the + is part of an expression. The generic form for the = operator is

```
<variable> = <numeric expression>.
```

When the goal containing the = is activated, the expression must be *evaluable*; that is, it must be possible for Turbo Prolog, following evaluation rules, to turn the expression into a numeric value. This means the expression cannot contain any uninstantiated variables or non-numeric constant values. The type of the value resulting from the evaluation of an expression depends on the type of the constants and variable and the operators in the expression.

The first thing that happens when an = predicate is activated is that the numeric expression is evaluated. In this example, 3 + 4 is evaluated to 7. Then one of two things happens. If the variable Sum is instantiated, the two values are compared, and if they match, the goal succeeds. For example, given the rule

```
check(Sum) :- Sum = 3 + 4.
Goal: check(7).
True
Goal: check(3).
False
```

If the variable is not instantiated, = instantiates it to the value from the expression.

```
Goal: check(What).
What = 7
1 solution
```

The expression may, and usually does, contain variables along with integers and operators. All variables in the expression, however, must have values before the = predicate is activated.

Numeric Expressions

The generic form for a numeric expression is

```
<numeric expression><infix operator><numeric expression>.
```

The standard selection for infix integer operators is:

+	addition	for integers and reals
—	subtraction	for integers and reals
*	multiplication	for integers and reals
/	division for quotient	always yields a real
mod	division for remainder	for integers
div	division for quotient	for integers

Addition, subtraction and multiplication are easy but the two kinds of division operators may deserve explanation. Integer arithmetic involves only whole numbers and division rarely "comes out even."

67 div 5 evaluates to 13	(the integer quotient from division)
67 mod 5 evaluates to 2	(the remainder from division)
15 mod 5 evaluates to 0	(the remainder from division)

Real division, the / operator, allows for decimal fractions in the result. It is like the division commonly done by calculators, etc.

To return to the generic form

```
<numeric expression><infix operator><numeric expression>.
```

we see that the arguments of the operator can be expressions themselves. For example,

```
2+3 * 4+6
```

This is ambiguous, however, as we cannot tell how the "sub-expressions" are meant to be grouped.

```
(2) + (3*4+6) or
(2+3) * (4+6)
(2+3*4) + (6)
```

There are two ways the ambiguity can be resolved. The first is to add in the parentheses that will group the expressions correctly. The second is to know and use the patterns written into the Turbo Prolog interpreter.

The patterns have standards in two areas, precedence and associativity. *Precedence* tells, given more than one kind of operator, which will be done first. Among these operators, mod and div have highest precedence, multiplication and division for quotient, which have the same precedence, are next, then add and subtract, which also have precedence equal to each other, are lowest. Complex expressions are evaluated according to these precedence rules.

Precedence Table

  mod, div
    * /
  + −

```
3 + 2 * 6          13 mod 3 - 1
3 + 12             1 - 1
15                 0
```

Associativity tells, given more than one operator of the same precedence, which will be done first. The precedence might be the same because the operators are in the same precedence class or because they are the same operator. All these operators are left associative, so under associativity, these operators will be done in the order they appear left to right.

```
6 * 6/2            4 + 3 - 1
36/2               7 - 1
18                 6

17 mod 3 mod 2     4/2/2
2 mod 2            2/2
0                  1
```

As a programming practice, it is better to use parentheses to group expressions, even if they are not necessary to force correct evaluation, because they help people understand the expression better and thus promote fewer errors.

Arithmetic often involves a mixture of real and integer values. In such cases, the arithmetic is done as though the integers were their real equivalents. The result is a real value. If the value is then instantiated to an integer type variable, the value will be truncated. That is, any fractional part of the number will be discarded.

```
predicates
    answer(integer)
clauses
    answer(Value) :- Value = 10/3.
```

```
Goal: answer(X).
X = 3
1 solution
```

The following example uses a database from which to do calculations.

```
predicates
    dimension(symbol,integer,integer,integer)
    floor(symbol,integer)
    wall(symbol,integer)
clauses
    dimension(living_room,15,18,12).
    dimension(kitchen,8,8,8).
    dimension(bed_room,10,12,8).
    floor(Room,Area)   :- dimension(Room,Wid,Len,Hig),
                          Area = Wid*Len.
    wall(Room,Area) :-
                  dimension(Room,Wid,Len,Hig),
                  Area = (2*(Wid*Hig))+(2*(Len*Hig)).
    Goal: floor(kitchen,Area).
    Area = 64
    1 solution
    Goal: wall(living_room,Space).
    Space = 792
    1 solution
```

EXERCISES 9.1

1. What will be the values for these expressions?

```
(2) + (3 * 4 + 6)
(2 + 3) * 4 + 6
(2 + 3 * 4) + 6 mod 2
```

2. Write a program that shows your answers in Exercise 1 agree with Turbo Prolog's evaluation.

9.2 COMPARING NUMERIC VALUES

A second way of making use of numbers is to compare values. One numeric value can be compared against another value, testing equal, greater or less than. The operators for these tests are built-in in Turbo Prolog.

=	equals
<>	does not equal
>	is greater than
<	is less than
>=	is greater than or equal
<=	is less than or equal

Note the operators that are made of two characters; the order in which the characters appear is important. They cannot be reversed.

Comparing directly against a number from a fact in the database provides direct comparisons. Variables can be instantiated to integers, as in this example which rates people according to their scores.

```
rating(Person,"ACE") :- score(Person,Points),
                                        Points>1000.
rating(Person,"NOVICE") :- score(Person,Points),
                                        Points<100.
rating(Person,"OK") :- score(Person,Points),
                        Points =< 1000, Points >= 100.
score(char,1100).


Goal: rating(char,Rate).
Rate = ACE
1 solution
Goal: rating(Who,"ACE").
Who = char
1 solution
```

Extracting Number Values

One appropriate use of arithmetic in Turbo Prolog is the analysis of a collection of facts in a database. Say we had a database with many facts of this form.

```
score(<person>,<points>).
```

We might, for example, want to find the average score for all people in the database. The attack this program takes is to gather all the scores into a list, then find the average from there.

```
score(char,1100).
:
average(Val) :- findall(N(score(_,N)),B),
                length(B,C),
                sum(B,T),
                Val = T/C.
length([ ],0).
length([_|T],S) :- length(T,R), S = R+1.
```

```
sum([ ],0).
sum([H|T],S) :- sum(T,R), S = R+H.
```

This program definition says that we can find the average score by gathering a list of the scores, getting the number of scores from the length of the list, summing up all the values in the list and then dividing the sum by the number. For finding the average we must be sure the total and the count have values so the average can be found. The last four lines of the database are the rules for finding these values.

Turbo Prolog provides a number of numeric functions that can be used in expressions or can be treated as individual expressions themselves. That is, they may be used in calculations and comparisons in the same way as expressions. These functions produce trigonometric values, square roots, logarithms and other numeric values. A list of these functions and the specifics of their use can be found in the Turbo Prolog Manual.

EXERCISES 9.3

1. Design facts and rules to calculate the average high temperature for a week.
2. Given a base of facts of the form

   ```
   person(<name>,<age>).
   ```

   write a rule to find out if one person is twice as old as another.
3. Using the database from Exercise 2, write a rule that would report everyone who is more than ten years older than a particular person.

9.3 USING ARITHMETIC IN DATA MANIPULATION

Many computer tasks focus on the processing of numbers. While other computer languages are much better for "number crunching," a programmer using Turbo Prolog may want to do some of these same tasks. One such task is sorting a set of number values into ascending order. Here, as an example, is a sort. This sort is called an insertion sort. It works by going to the tail of a list, then moving backward toward the head of the list, taking each element in turn and putting it into the tail in the place it belongs.

```
domains
    list = integer*
predicates
    ins_sort(list,list)
    insert(integer,list,list)
clauses
    ins_sort([ ],[ ]).
```

```
ins_sort([Head|Tail],New_list) :-
        ins_sort(Tail,New_tail),
        insert(Head,New_tail,New_list).
insert(Elem,[Val|List1],[Val|List2] :-
        Elem >= Val, !,
        insert(Elem,List1,List2).
insert(Elem,List,[Elem|List]).
Goal: ins_sort([3,9,6],Result).
Result = [3,6,9]
1 solution
```

The predicate, insert, works by moving down the list to find the place for the new element. It moves as long as the element is greater than the head of the list. When the comparison fails, the correct location for the new element has been discovered. Because the original list is sorted, the remainder beyond this location belongs beyond the element to be inserted. The second part of the insert definition enters the element in the list.

In many problems, the programmer would like to have some random variation of values that are used as part of the program. For example, in game playing, the value of an integer may determine a move and a variety of moves may be what makes the game interesting. Turbo Prolog has built-in a predicate that will produce a number that can be used for simulating randomness. The predicate, called random, is activated with an uninstantiated variable and returns a real number between zero and one or equal to zero.

```
Goal: random(X).
X = .23430142679
1 solution
```

EXERCISES 9.3

1. How could ins_sort be modified to sort numbers into decreasing instead of increasing order?
2. How would ins_sort's behavior be different if >= were replaced by > ?
3. What would be required to make ins_sort sort constant names?

9.4 AN ARITHMETIC EXAMPLE

Suppose we have a Turbo Prolog database that contains information about the presidents of the United States as facts of the form:

```
president(<name>,<birth year>,
          <year began office>,<year left office>).
```

From this base, we can derive several kinds of information.

How long a president was in office:

```
length_office(Name,Years) :-
           president(Name,_,In,Out), Years = Out-In.
```

How old a particular president was when he took office:

```
age(Name,Years)  :- president(Name,Birth,In,_),
                    Years = In-Birth.
```

Which president was a certain age when he took office:

same rule, switch variables in the question.
use age(Who,55) instead of age(johnson,What).

Which president was younger than fifty when he took office:

```
young(Name) :- president(Name,Birth,In,_),
               Years = In-Birth, Years<=50.
```

Which president served a part term:

```
fractional(Name) :- president(Name,_,In,Out),
                    Part = (Out-In) mod 4, Part <> 0.
```

Who was president in a certain year:

```
in_office(Name,Year) :- president(Name,_,In,Out),
                        Year <= Out, Year >= In.
```

This is the first of the two-argument rules in this arithmetic section that cannot be used in the reverse direction.

```
Goal: in_office(kennedy,1962).
True
Goal: in_office(Who,1955).
Who = eisenhower
1 solution
Goal: in_office(kennedy,When).
Error: free variable in expression
```

This error occurred because the variable, When, was uninstantiated instead of having a value. When a comparison was made, the lack of a value caused an error. Such errors as these are easy to make when doing arithmetic. The programmer must be alert to the bias that evaluation has as part of its structure.

SUMMARY

Turbo Prolog provides facility to do arithmetic, using predefined operators for doing calculations and for comparing values. Expressions are evaluated when the operator predicates are activated; numeric variables can then be instantiated to those values.

EXERCISES CHAPTER 9 ━━━━━━━━━━

1. What will be Turbo Prolog's evaluation and resulting type for these expressions?

   ```
   (3 + 4) mod 2.
   (3 + 4) / 2.
   (3 + 4) div 2.
   ```

2. How will Turbo Prolog respond to these goals?

   ```
   Goal: V= 3, V<3.
   Goal: V= 3, V<=3.
   Goal: V<= 3, V=3.
   ```

3. Write Turbo Prolog programs for these six problems.

   a) Given an integer greater than zero, use a formula to find the sum of all the integers starting with 1 and ending with the integer given. If the integer is called N, the formula to find this sum is

   $$\frac{N * (N + 1)}{2}$$

   b) Write another solution to the same problem, this time recursively adding the numbers up to N. That is, the sum for N is the same as the sum for N − 1 with N added to it.

   c) Make up a database of costs of items in a store, such as a clothing store. Write rules to find the total cost for several items and one to calculate a 20% discount.

   d) The factorial of a number is defined to be the product of all the integers starting with 1, continuing up to the number. Recursively, the factorial of a number (say 5) is found by multiplying the number times the factorial of the next lower integer (here 4; 4 factorial is 24, 5 factorial is 120). Write a recursive rule for factorial, using the stopping case of 1 factorial being 1.

   e) Modify your factorial rule to protect it against receiving an argument less than 1.

   f) A count of the number of elements in a list is commonly called the length of the list. Write a recursive rule that finds the length of a given list.

10

Building Larger Programs

The purpose of this chapter is to help the learner:

- understand how programs can be developed in modules.
- learn to use problem solving tactics.
- be familiar with debugging tactics, general and Turbo Prolog specific.
- consider programming style issues such as
    name choices and physical layout.
    documentation.
    ease of use and robustness.

10.1 DESIGNING PROGRAMS

As programs get larger they contain more and different ideas that the programmer has to put together. Parts of programs are related to or dependent on other parts, and with a large number of parts, interconnectedness results in increased complexity. If one particular part, say a multiple-definition predicate, is subtle in the way it works, any confusion it causes to people reading it may carry over to confusion about the rest of the program.

These factors, length, interconnectedness, and subtlety all add to the *cognitive complexity* of a program. Programs that are large and handle significant problems are bound to be more complex than short ones that do trivial problems.

Complexity, however, makes programs harder to write, more apt to have errors, and harder to discover any errors in. It also makes it harder for a person to read and understand a program. The person reading the program might be an individual who is not the one who wrote the program or it might be the programmer, who, after some length of time, goes back to reuse the program.

To reduce these problems, programmers can follow some established software development practices. These practices, which are also used by programmers who write in other programming languages, fall into two general categories: structure and style.

Modularity

The main goal in good program structure is modularity. *Modularity* means that a program is made up of units separated according to the function they handle. Turbo Prolog includes a system facility to allow the construction of large programs by actually building and compiling component modules separately, then executing them as a group. Each of the modules is its own complete program that can be designed, constructed and tested separately. Then one main program is built that uses the preconstructed modules. The domains, predicates and clauses declarations that are part of each of the modules are encapsulated in the modules. *Encapsulation* means each module has exclusive access to its own domains, predicates and clauses. Communication between different modules is handled by a special set of global domains and predicates.

In addition to reducing the complexity of designing large programs, separate module construction and encapsulation has two other advantages:

1. different people can work on different parts independently;
2. modules that have been created for a specific purpose can be reused in other subsequent programming tasks.

The modularity allowed by this system facility is important for high-level organization of large programs. But even at a much lower level, Turbo Prolog has some modularity inherent in its structure. A Turbo Prolog sentence has the function of defining the term that is the head of the sentence. For example,

```
mono_feet(Hue) :- color(Footgear,Hue),
                  shade(sox,Hue).
```

One Turbo Prolog sentence cannot define more than one term, as only one term can be in the head of the sentence.

Frequently, of course, we need a multiple rule definition for a term.

```
append([ ],L,L).
append([H|L1],L2,[H|L3]) :- append(L1,L2,L3).
```

These two sentences between them define append.

Similarly, a group of facts with the same predicate defines the meaning of that predicate by declaring all the cases where it is true.

```
weather(monday,fair).
weather(tuesday,cloudy).
```

These three examples, the simple rule, the multiple rule and the group of facts, show the fundamental units from which Turbo Prolog programs are built.

Looking at rules, we recognize that the terms in the body of the rules sometimes include terms that are references to other definitions. For example the mono_feet rule makes reference to color and shade as part of its definition. For the mono_feet rule to be functional, the definitions of color and shade must also be available.

From these examples, we can see that, conceptually, modules exist from the very-small rule level up through the complete program level.

Larger modules are built of smaller modules. In Chapter 5, for example, we saw a module

```
palindrome(Half,Whole) :- reverse(Half,Rest),
                             append(Half,Rest,Whole).
```

The palindrome module is made up of this rule, the reverse module and the append module. Modules form a hierarchy in which higher units are lower units aggregated together. In general, a module consists of a rule that defines some function and the rules that define the terms that appear in the body of the rule.

Bottom Up and Top Down

Continuing this process of building modules on modules, we see that a program, however large, is built of smaller modules. Creating a program by building modules, then integrating them in larger modules, is called *bottom-up* programming.

Rarely, however, do we use this method by itself to write a program. Bottom-up programming lends itself to exploration and serendipity, while most programming is focused on a specific objective. When we write a significant program, our task is to solve a problem that is expressed at the top of the hierarchy. To get from this starting point down to the fundamental units that the structure is built on, we use a process called *top-down design*. The purpose of top-down design is to give the programmer a clear understanding of the program, its component parts and the way those components fit together.

In working top-down, a critical part of the strategy is to be willing to put off consideration of specific details when larger units are being considered. One tactic that is often helpful in supporting focus on units rather than detail is to draw a diagram.

Say we were working on a program that accepted a question and returned an answer, with the question and answer in English sentences. At the top level we could diagram this program as in Figure 10.1.

At this level, we need not concern ourselves with details of the modules in the bottom level of the diagram. We do need to be sure the modules below add up to the one above and we should be concerned about communication between the modules. We might improve the diagram by writing in the arguments for each definition along the communication lines as in Figure 10.2.

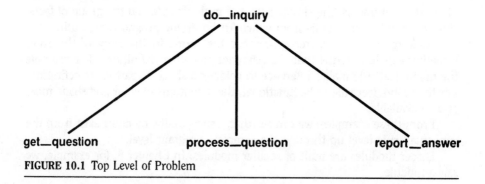

FIGURE 10.1 Top Level of Problem

From Figure 10.2, we can write the rule for the module that is the whole program unit.

```
do_inquiry :- get_question(Query),
               process_question(Query,Answer),
               report_answer(Answer).
```

There is more to this module, however, as definitions of the three component modules are needed. These can be designed top-down, too. For example, see Figure 10.3.

The module for getting a string of characters from the user involves getting the first printing character and then getting characters repeatedly until the character that indicates the end is found. Similar analysis of the other modules to process the question and to repeat the answer would also be done. There is nothing magic about the particular diagrams shown here. Individual people will have particular kinds of diagrams and notational systems they find helpful. Using some kind of diagram does, however, facilitate the programmer's understanding of the problem by focusing attention on the component modules and the relationship between parts of the modules.

Advantages of Modularity

Top-down design helps the programmer comprehend and develop the modularity in a program. This reductionistic approach to problem solving can benefit both the effectiveness and the efficiency of a programmer's effort.

Most important, it limits the complexity of what the programmer must be able to think about at one time. Ignoring the details of one module while working on another saves cognitive load. In a like manner, the independence of modules allows more than one programmer to work on a program, with individuals building modules to fit together according to the definition given for a higher-level module.

Another advantage of modularity is that modules, once written, can be used again in other programs that include the same component. The module that is

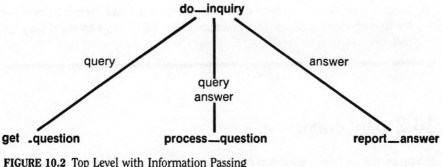

FIGURE 10.2 Top Level with Information Passing

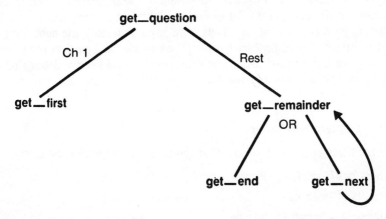

FIGURE 10.3 Get Question Module

specified above, get_question, is like a program developed in Chapter 8. It can be used in this program, sparing the programmer its rewriting.

A final and very useful facet of modules is that they can be written into Turbo Prolog and tested independent of other modules. For example, the palindrome program could be written in three steps: the append module written and tested; the reverse module written and tested; the palindrome rule added, creating the top-level module, and the whole tested. In this process we have returned to do bottom-up programming guided by our top-down design.

EXERCISES 10.1 ━━━━━━━━━━━━━━━━━━━━━━━━━━━

1. Diagram a top-down design for a well-balanced meal.
2. Diagram a top-down design for palindromes with an uneven number of letters.

3. Given a procedure to do even-numbered palindromes and the one from above for uneven-numbered, write a procedure to check strings to see if they are palindromes.

10.2 DEBUGGING

If a programmer does a good top-down design and an accurate translation of the design into Turbo Prolog, the resulting program will not have errors in it. Errors, which in programming are called *bugs,* do in reality appear.

Bugs can result from errors in the design of the program or from incorrect translation of the design into Turbo Prolog. Debugging a program is usually an interesting problem-solving task itself. It requires observing the behavior of the program, inferring relationships between the behavior and parts of the program, hypothesizing a correction and testing the correction. Effective debugging concentrates on the first two of these four steps rather than the last two.

Observing Program Behavior

There are three sources of information about how a program is behaving:

- messages from Turbo Prolog
- results of test cases
- traces of program executions

Messages from Turbo Prolog are most apparent. Some messages indicate that the compiler found some character in the program that did not fit the syntax rules. Similarly, messages about running out of space or not being able to read from a specified file provide the programmer with information that may point toward the bug. Error messages are sometimes distractors, however, because the actual error might occur earlier than where the system recognized a problem. For example, the first time the programmer keyed in the module from Chapter 9 that does insertion sort, it looked like this

```
clauses
    ins_sort([ ],[ ]).
    ins_sort([Head|Tail],[New_list]) :-
            ins_sort(Tail,New_tail),
            insert(Head,New_tail,New_list).
    insert(Elem,[Val|List1],[Val|List2]) :-
            Elem >= Val, !,
            insert(Elem,List1,List2).
    insert(Elem,L,[Elem|L]).
```

The compiler reported a

```
2205 Type error: illegal variable type
          for this predicate
```

and put the cursor under New_list in the insert sub-goal of ins_sort (line 4). Careful checking in the domains and predicates section for insert's definition did not uncover the source of the problem. A wider search finally found the difficulty, a spare set of brackets around New_list in the head of the rule defining ins_sort.

After the fact, it is easy to see that the original message derived from the error above it. Like many a puzzle, the answer is obvious once you know the answer.

Trying various test cases is a powerful way of pinning down a bug. When a module contains a multiple rule, only part of the cases may use the rule with the problem, so varying test cases may focus attention on the buggy definition. Trying test cases and observing results allows elimination of areas where the bug is not. This is an example of a standard problem-solving technique, using inference to limit the search space.

Another standard debugging tactic is to trace the process of the program execution. Programs can be traced by hand, with the programmer simulating the machine under control of the program. The programmer follows the flow of control, noting instantiations and backtracking as appropriate. The problem with hand simulations is that the programmer is apt to do what he or she knows the program should do rather than what it in fact would do.

It is more effective to let the system report the actual flow of control and instantiations during a program execution. This is usually very helpful because the programmer knows how the trace should look and any divergence is immediately apparent.

A full trace, as we saw in Chapter 4, shows all the goals that were activated and resulting successes and failures. The problem with a machine trace is usually too much information. Turbo Prolog allows us to limit the trace to some predicates or some segments of the execution, turning the trace on and off. We then are given information only about the specified components. To choose the correct segments, of course, the programmer must have at least some idea where the problem might be. This is another reason for building and testing a program in modules.

Tracing is not only useful in debugging; it is also a good learning tool. Watching a trace of Turbo Prolog processing can be edifying especially if the control pattern is complex. As an auxiliary to a trace, drawing diagrams is frequently helpful. For example, Figure 10.4 shows the execution of the rule to get a string from the user.

A last and very important debugging tactic is to take a break from looking for the bug. In deducing the relationships between program parts and program behavior, premature conclusions often interfere with the problem solving. Taking a break can allow a new start. Explaining to another person what the program is supposed to be doing is another way of discovering a program bug, especially

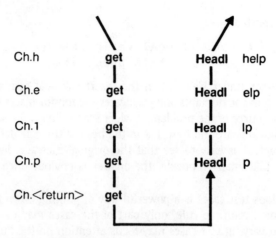

FIGURE 10.4 Execution of Get_string

a logic error. The person hearing the explanation does not need to understand the program; it is in the explaining that the programmer discovers where the bug arose.

Debugging Database Modifiers

When a program uses procedures that modify the contents of the database, all the planning and modular testing can go awry. The modules that have been built and tested may no longer be trustworthy if modifications of the database are made. To try to control entry of bugs in programs that use these "meta-logical" predicates they should be kept as non-pervasive as possible and their use should be carefully documented

EXERCISES 10.2

1. Hand trace the execution of the goal, based on these rules.

```
length([],0).
length([_|T],S) :- length(T,R), S = R + 1.
Goal: length([8,6,3],Size).
```

2. Say you had this rule

```
palindrome(List1,List2) :-
         append(List1,List3,List2),
         reverse(List1,List3).
```

and got this result

```
Goal: palindrome([a,b],Result)
Result = [a,b,a,b,b]
```

what would be some test cases that might help discover the bug?

10.3 DOCUMENTATION

The previous discussion in this chapter has to do with the structure of larger programs. Documentation is one of the facets of programming *style* that is important in writing larger programs. Documentation is a commentary about the program. Programs usually have internal documentation and external documentation.

Internal documentation consists of comments that are written in the Turbo Prolog program to give a human reader information about the program. Particular procedures such as predicates that modify the database or uses of cut that eliminate certain options should be noted. Modules should be labeled according to their function.

Because we cannot simply add comments into a program as if they were Turbo Prolog sentences, special marks are provided to enclose these comments, the /*...*/ brackets.

```
'*This comment will be ignored by Turbo Prolog*/
```

The Turbo Prolog system simply skips over any characters between the marks. Note that this introduces a new source of bugs: commenting out definitions by mistake.

External documentation usually contains a description of what the program is for, how to use it and any special characteristics a programmer might need to know about it. It may be in the form of books and manuals, in the form of document files on a system or in the form of introductory information as part of the program, explaining its use. External documentation is important to the long-term value of a program. If a program is going to be used as part of another program or revised with modification, documentation provides the vehicle for knowing how.

Name Choices

The amount of internal documentation needed to make clear the purpose of program components depends on how the names for constants and variables are chosen. Well-chosen names can communicate a good deal of information to a human using or reading a program. From Turbo Prolog's point of view, these two definitions are equivalent.

```
a(X,Y) :- b(X,M),c(Y,M).
uncle(Man,Child) :- brother(Man,Person),
                    parent(Child,Person).
```

The human readers who gain from the communication inherent in well-chosen names include the original programmer.

User-defined Domains

We have used the domains section of our programs to define structured types of variables. The domains section also allows us to define specifically named types that are based on the standard types. For example, we might name two symbol types called people and houses.

```
domains
    people, houses = symbol
predicates
    live_in(people,houses)
    on_street(houses)
clauses
    live_in(joe,Structure) :- on_street(Structure).
    on_street(mansion).
```

The compiler checks to see that variables match the correct domain each time they appear in the rule. Thus if we made a mistake and reversed the two arguments in the rule

```
live_in(Structure,joe) :- on_street(Structure).
```

the compiler would object that there is a type mismatch in the rule.

Type checking is an important means through which the computer system can help the programmer ensure that the program is correct. At the minimum level, the compiler checks to be sure we are not, for example, adding together two symbols or trying to separate a number into characters. Using the domain declarations to name types adds an additional level of security and also allows us to use meaningful names in the predicates declaration.

When we define a type based on one of the standard domain types, the user-defined type inherits all the characteristics of the base type. In our example above, people and houses are based on symbols, so they can be treated like symbols, using all the built-in predicates and input/output facilities that are used for symbols.

Defining our own named types adds a certain amount of work to the process of writing a program but it provides us with an extra check on the correctness of the program we have written. The compiler does another check on the arguments of predicates, concerning the instantiation sequence. When a series of sub-goals will be activated, we normally expect arguments from the earlier goals to all be instantiated before the processing moves on to the next goal. In declarative programming, this expected sequence is not actually necessary. An uninstantiated variable may be associated with another uninstantiated variable and simply held pending until some later action instantiates them both.

If the compiler finds an uninstantiated argument being passed along to another goal, it will generate a warning. The warning can be overridden with F10 or prevented by adding the nowarnings compiler directive to the top of the database. More positively, the argument type can be defined in the domains section to be of *reference* type, which specifies that the passing as an uninstantiated argument is anticipated.

Physical Layout

Another characteristic of programming style is the physical layout of the clauses. The two most important rules-of-thumb in program layout are to be consistent and to use empty space generously. Modules should be written as units with blank lines between modules. If a module is quite large, then its component modules should also be set off with blank lines. "Quite large" is a very subjective term; twenty facts of the same form is not as large a unit as twenty complex rules.

The physical layout of rules will depend on the complexity of the requirements and the length of the terms. Since rules rarely fit entirely on one line, some decision must be made about where the requirements will be listed. Continuation to the next line, with or without indentation, is one possibility. Another is listing only one term per line, so the requirements form a column on the page.

In general, if a rule has more than five or six requirements in its body, there should probably be another intermediate level of modules in between the rule and the requirements.

Well-written Programs

In addition to having good structure and style, well-written programs are easy to use. Being easy to use includes providing instruction at the level needed by the user, and being robust enough so that a small error by the user does not result in disaster.

Structure, style and other design decisions depend on the individual who is programming the problem solution. Different people prefer different structure and style patterns. Programmers will also be forced to make tradeoffs on desirable program characteristics. For example, speed of response may be lost as more humane user interfaces are built. Nonetheless, the programmer must be aware of these concerns.

EXERCISES 10.3 ■■■■■■■■■

1. Rewrite these clauses with good physical arrangement and documentation.

```
rev([ ],[ ]).
app([ ],X,X).
palin(X,X2) :- app(X,L3,X2), rev(X,L3).
rev([H|T],L) :- rev(T,Out), app(Out,[H],L).
app([E|X],X2,[E|L3]) :- app(X,X2,L3).
```

2. Break this rule up into three components and write a rule to call the components.

```
have_groceries :- cereal(Brand),
                  juice(Fruit),
                  caffeine(Drink),
                  sandwich(Filling),
                  milk(white),
                  supper_dish(Pasta),
                  pie(Type).
```

3. Add one more requirement to have_groceries, that Fruit is not instantiated to the same constant as Type, and rewrite the have_groceries rule you wrote in Exercise 2 to handle this.

10.4 AN EXAMPLE OF PROGRAM DEVELOPMENT

A typical programming project starts out with an ill-defined problem. The problem must be explored and clarified before the top-down analysis can be done.

Problem:

We want an editor that replaces jargon with non-technical words.

Clarification: is there a one-to-one replacement list for the jargon and non-technical equivalents? Yes.

Clarification: what units will be handled? Sentences.

Clarification: where will the sentences come from? The user.

Clarification: where will the edited sentences be reported? The user.

Clarification: should the user interface include prompts or a comment along with the answer? Just "Type in a sentence." and "The edited sentence is:".

Clarification: how is the sentence delineated? Ends with a period.

Clarification: will the sentence be more than one line long? No.

Clarification: should I worry about commas and other special symbols? Not this time.

Preliminary breakdown of the problem:
> get the string
> make changes
> display the changed string

Decision: internal representation for the changing module will have words as items in a list.

Decision: the input module will be responsible for changing the character input to tokens. For symmetry, the display module will take care of format from the token form.

Analysis of the middle module:

Go down the list, switching words to be edited out for their replacements. Work recursively to the end. Any word without a replacement just gets copied.

Decide to build this part and test it.
Recursive rule needs stopping case.

```
new_form([ ],[ ]).
new_form([Old|Tail],[New|New_tail]) :-
          swap(Old,New),
          new_form(Tail,New_tail).
```

A set of facts of the form swap(<old>,<new>) will specify each of the jargon words and its replacement.

To handle words not changed, return same value; put non-change rule at bottom of list so any change rules encountered first.

```
swap(Any,Any).
```

Write the module, provide a few words to swap and test.

```
domains
   words = symbol
   wordlist = words*
predicates
   swap(words,words)
   new_form(wordlist,wordlist)
clauses
   swap(groovy,exciting) :- !.
   swap(ugly,unattractive) :- !.
   swap(Any,Any).
   new_form([],[]).
   new_form([Old|Tail],[New|New_tail]) :-
             swap(Old,New), new_form(Tail,New_tail).
Goal: new_form([this,is,groovy],Result).
Result = [this is exciting]
1 solution
```

Analysis of input module:

The input module includes prompting the user, getting the input and transforming it into a list of words. The transformation to words is an extension of a component developed in Chapter 7.

```
domains
    words = symbol
    wordlist = words*
predicates
    inquire(wordlist)
    prompt
    sentence(wordlist)
    reform(string,string)
    break_up(string,wordlist)
clauses
    inquire(List) :- prompt, sentence(List).
    prompt :-    write("Please enter a sentence."),nl.
    sentence(Units) :- readln(Sentence),
                        reform(Sentence,LC_form),
                        break_up(LC_form,Units).
    reform(Original,LC_form) :-
                        frontstr(1,Original,First,Rest),
                        upper_lower(First,New_first),
                        concat(New_first,Rest,LC_form).
    break_up(".",[]) :- !.
    break_up(String,[Part|U_tail]) :-
                        fronttoken(String,Part,S_tail),
                        break_up(S_tail,U_tail).
Goal: sentence(What).
Please enter a sentence.
This is it.
What = [this,is,it]
1 solution
```

Analysis of output module:

The output comment is done in the same manner as the prompt in the input. The sentence is rebuilt as a string from the words, adding capitalization and a period. The rebuild rule is recursive with the stopping case of a list with only one element in it.

```
domains
    words = symbol
    wordlist = words*
predicates
    show(wordlist)
```

```
      comment
      respond(wordlist)
      rebuild(wordlist,string)
      complete(string,string)
   clauses
      show(Result) :- comment, respond(Result).
      comment :- nl,
               write("The edited sentence is: "), nl.
      respond(Result) :- rebuild(Result,Out_form),
                         complete(Out_form,Out_string),
                         write(Out_string), nl.
      rebuild([Single],Last_word) :-
                   fronttoken(Last_word,Single,""), !.
      rebuild([Word|T_tail],S_form) :-
                 rebuild(T_tail,Tail_string),
                 concat(" ",Tail_string,Spaced_string),
                 fronttoken(S_form,Word,Spaced_string).
      complete(Plain,Finished) :-
               frontstr(1,Plain,First,Rest),
               upper_lower(New_first,First),
               concat(New_first,Rest,Intermed),
               concat(Intermed,".",Finished).
   Goal: show([this,one]).
   The edited sentence is:
   This one.
   1 solution
```

Specification of the top-level module:

The components are all combined and an internal goal is added for the top-level execution.

```
goal
   inquire(Sentence),
   new_form(Sentence,Result),
   show(Result).
```

The final program, ready to have the dictionary specified with the needed vocabulary:

```
domains
   words = symbol
   wordlist = words*

predicates
   swap(words,words)
   new_form(wordlist,wordlist)
   inquire(wordlist)
```

```
    prompt
    sentence(wordlist)
    reform(string,string)
    break_up(string,wordlist)
    show(wordlist)
    comment
    respond(wordlist)
    rebuild(wordlist,string)
    complete(string,string)

clauses
    /*  edit module and dictionary  */

    swap(groovy,exciting) :- !.
    swap(ugly,unattractive) :- !.
    swap(Any,Any).
    new_form([ ],[ ]).
    new_form([Old|Tail],[New|New_tail]) :-
            swap(Old,New), new_form(Tail,New_tail).

    /*  input module  */

    inquire(List) :- prompt, sentence(List).
    prompt :- write("Please enter a sentence."),nl.

    sentence(Units) :- readln(Sentence),
                    reform(Sentence,LC_form),
                    break_up(LC_form,Units).
    reform(Original,LC_form) :-
                frontstr(1,Original,First,Rest),
                upper_lower(First,New_first),
                concat(New_first,Rest,LC_form).
    break_up(".",[]) :- !.
    break_up(String,[Part|U_tail]) :-
                    fronttoken(String,Part,S_tail),
                    break_up(S_tail,U_tail).

    /*  output module  */

    show(Result) :- comment, respond(Result).
    comment :-
            nl, write("The edited sentence is:"), nl.
    respond(Result) :- rebuild(Result,Out_form),
                    complete(Out_form,Out_string),
                    write(Out_string), nl.
```

```
rebuild([Single],Last_word) :-
            fronttoken(Last_word,Single,""), !.
rebuild([Word|T_tail],S_form) :-
            rebuild(T_tail,Tail_string),
            concat(" ",Tail_string,Spaced_string),
            fronttoken(S_form,Word,Spaced_string).
complete(Plain,Finished) :-
            frontstr(1,Plain,First,Rest),
            upper_lower(New_first,First),
            concat(New_first,Rest,Intermed),
            concat(Intermed,".",Finished).

    /*  main definition  */

goal
    inquire(Sentence),
    new_form(Sentence,Result),
    show(Result).
```

SUMMARY

Large programs are built out of modules which, in Turbo Prolog, are smaller programs themselves. Careful analysis of the problem that we want the program to solve leads to a well structured program.

Program style has the fundamental goal of clearly communicating the program's function to people who will be reading or using the program. A program should be as easy to use as is possible within the other constraints under which the program developer must work.

EXERCISES CHAPTER 10 ━━━━━━━━━━━━━━━━━━

1 Write programs for these problems.

a) A concordance is a listing of words that occur in a text along with a count of the frequency of each word. The words are listed in alphabetical order. Write a program to produce a concordance from a list of words presented as Turbo Prolog strings.

b) Write a program to play tic-tac-toe. For a simple version, have Turbo Prolog play second and only play a defensive game.

c) Write a program that understands simple sentences of the forms:

_____ is a _____.

A _____ is a _____.

Is _____ a _____?

The program should respond to the questions according to the previously given sentences.

d) Layout a map of 5 cities, then write a program that plans the route between two towns (entered by user) and reports a route and the total mileage. A simple version would find any one route; a more complex one would find the best route.

Appendixes

ASCII Codes

AMERICAN STANDARD CODE FOR INFORMATION INTERCHANGE

0	NUL	Null	29	GS	Group separator	58	:
1	SOH	Start heading	30	RS	Record separator	59	;
2	STX	Start text	31	US	Unit separator	60	<
3	ETX	End text	32	SP	Space	61	=
4	EOT	End transmission	33	!		62	)
5	ENQ	Inquiry	34	"		63	?
6	ACK	Acknowledgment	35	#		64	@
7	BEL	Bell	36	$		65	A
8	BS	Backspace	37	%		66	B
9	HT	Horizontal tab	38	&		67	C
10	LF	Line feed	39	'		68	D
11	VT	Vertical tab	40	(		69	E
12	FF	Form feed	41	)		70	F
13	CR	Carriage return	42	*		71	G
14	SO	Shift out	43	+		72	H
15	SI	Shift in	44	,		73	I
16	DLE	Data link escape	45	–		74	J
17	DC1	Device control 1	46	.		75	K
18	DC2	Device control 2	47	/		76	L
19	DC3	Device control 3	48	0		77	M
20	DC4	Device control 4	49	1		78	N
21	NAK	Neg. acknowledge	50	2		79	O
22	SYN	Synchronous/Idle	51	3		80	P
23	ETB	End trans. block	52	4		81	Q
24	CAN	Cancel data	53	5		82	R
25	EM	End of medium	54	6		83	S
26	SUB	Start special seq. (eof)	55	7		84	T
27	ESC	Escape	56	8		85	U
28	FS	File separator	57	9		86	V

87	W	101	e	115	s	
88	X	102	f	116	t	
89	Y	103	g	117	u	
90	Z	104	h	118	v	
91	[	105	i	119	w	
92	\	106	j	120	x	
93	]	107	k	121	y	
94	↑	108	l	122	z	
95	—	109	m	123	{	
96	`	110	n	124	|	
97	a	111	o	125	}	
98	b	112	p	126	~	
99	c	113	q	127	DEL	
100	d	114	r			

Appendix B

Further Reading

Apt, K. R. and van Emden, M. H. Contributions to the theory of logic programming. *Journal of ACM* 29, 841–862, 1982.

Backus, J. Can programming be liberated from the von Neumann style? *Communications of the ACM*, 21, 613–641, 1978.

Borland. *Turbo Prolog Owner's Handbook*. Borland, Int. Scotts Valley, CA, 1986 (version 3).

Bratko, I. *Prolog Programming for Artificial Intelligence*. Addison-Wesley, Wokingham, England, 1986.

Clark, K. L. and McCabe, F. G. *Micro-Prolog: Programming in Logic*. Prentice-Hall, Englewood Cliffs, NJ, 1984.

Clark, K. L. and Tarnlund, S. A. (Editors) *Logic Programming* (APIC Studies in Data Processing, Vol. 16). Academic Press, London, 1982.

Clocksin, W. F. and Mellish, C. S. *Programming in Prolog* (second edition). Springer-Verlag, Berlin, 1984.

Coelho, H., Cotta, J. and Pereira, L. *How To Solve With Prolog* (second edition). Universidade Nova de Lisboa, Portugal, 1980.

Conery, J. S. and Kibler, D. F. Parallel interpretaton of logic programs. *Proc. ACM Conference on Functional Programming Languages and Computer Architecture*. Portsmouth, NH, 1981.

Ennals, R. *Beginning Micro-Prolog*. Harper and Row, New York, 1984.

Deliyanni, A. and Kowalski, R. A. Logic and semantic networks. *Communications of the ACM* 22, 184–192, 1979.

Feigenbaum, E. and McCorduck, P. *The Fifth Generation*. Signet, New York, 1984.

Giannesini, F., Kanoui, H., Pasero, R. and van Caneghen, M. *Prolog*. Addison-Wesley, Wokingham, England, 1986.

Harris, M. D. *An Introduction to Natural Language Processing*. Reston, Reston, VA, 1985.

Journal of Logic Programming. North Holland, New York, July 1984—ongoing.

Hoare, C. A. R. An axiomatic basis for computer programming. *Communications of the ACM* 12, 576–580, 1969.

Hogger, C. J. Derivation of logic programs. *Journal of the ACM* 28, 372–422, 1981.

Hogger, C. J. *Introduction to Logic Programming* (APIC Studies in Data Processing, Vol. 21). Academic Press, London, 1984.

International Symposium on Logic Programming. Atlantic City, NJ. IEEE Computer Society Press, New York, 1984.

International Symposium on Logic Programming. Boston, IEEE Computer Society Press, New York, 1985.

Kowalski, R. A. *Logic for Problem Solving*. Elsevier-North Holland, New York, 1979.

Kowalski, R. A. Algorithm = logic + control. *Communications of the ACM* 22, 424–436, 1979.

Li, D. *A PROLOG Database System*. John Wiley and Sons, New York, 1984.

Lloyd, J. W. *Foundations of Logic Programming*. Springer-Verlag, Berlin, 1984.

Pereira, L. M. (ed). *Logic Programming Newsletter*. Universidade Nova de Lisboa, Portugal, 1981—ongoing.

Rich, E. *Artificial Intelligence*. McGraw-Hill, New York, 1983.

Robinson, J. A. A machine-oriented logic based on the resolution principle. *Journal of ACM* 12, 23–41, 1965.

Robinson, J. A. *Logic: Form and Function*. Elsevier-North Holland, New York, 1979.

Sterling, L. and Shapiro, E. *The Art of Prolog*. MIT Press, Cambridge, MA, 1986.

Warren, D. H. D., Pereira, L. M., and Pereira, F. C. N. PROLOG-the language and its implementation compared with LISP. *Proc. of Symposium on Artificial Intelligence and Programming Languages, SIGPLAN Notices*, 12:8, 1977.

Wos, L., Overbeek, R., Lusk, E. and Boyle, J. *Automated Reasoning*. Prentice-Hall, Englewood Cliffs, NJ, 1984.

Comparison of Different Versions of Prolog

Two important ways that all these versions of Prolog are different from Turbo Prolog are 1) Turbo Prolog is strongly-typed, 2) Turbo Prolog has a far more extensive and better integrated programming environment.

A number of people have written interpreters so that Prolog is available on a wide variety of computers. These interpreters fall into two general categories, those in the Standard Prolog family and those in the micro-Prolog family.

Four of the most common versions of Prolog or micro-Prolog are compared in this section, two from each family. They are:

Edinburgh syntax, based on the original implementation, DECsystem-10/20, very close to Turbo Prolog syntax with only a few differences;

C-Prolog, very similar to Edinburgh, designed for 32-bit machines such as the VAX;

micro-Prolog, written specifically for microcomputers, using a syntax somewhat different from Edinburgh;

SIMPLE, an extension of micro-Prolog, designed to use a more English-like syntax.

The syntax described in the four sections appears in the order that syntax is introduced in the text, chapter by chapter.

Note: DECsystem-10 and VAX are trademarks of Digital Equipment Corporation.

EDINBURGH SYNTAX PROLOG

Chapter 2

Facts	predicate(arguments).
example	`likes(sally,swimming).`
	`friendly(sally).`
	`shops(sally,vegetables,market).`
Constants	begin with a lower-case letter
example	`sally`
Variables	begin with an upper-case letter
example	`Sport`
Query (goal)	clause with or without variables follows a ?-
example	`?- likes(sally,swimming).`
single answer	respond with a return
example	`?- likes(sally,Sport).`
	`Sport = swimming`
	`yes`
multiple answer	respond with a semi-colon
example	`?- likes(sally,Sport).`
	`Sport = swimming ;`
	`Sport = tennis ;`
	`no`
Conjunctions	use a comma for "and"
example	`?- likes(Who,swimming),`
	`         brought(Who,suit).`
Creating a database	access Prolog, get prompt |?-
from user (to interac-	`consult(user).` or `[user].`
tively build database)	CONTROL Z to stop
example	`|?- [user].`
	`|likes(sally,swimming).`
	`|^Z`
	`|?-`
from file (previously	`consult('<file-name>').` or
built by editor or	`    ['<file-name>'].`
saved from past session)	
example	`['star.2'].`
	`STAR.2 CONSULTED`

Chapter 3

Rule	<head> :- <body>.
example	`gets_exercise(Who) :-`
	`    likes(Who,swimming).`

Rules with conjunction	use comma for conjunction

example	`gets_exercise(Who) :-`
	`    likes(Who,swimming),`
	`    brought(Who,suit).`

Interrupt	^C CONTROL C

Chapter 4

Trace	facility to observe processing
example	`?- trace.` `?- get_exercise(Who).`

Chapter 5

List	collection of objects specified in order
example	`[bank,store,florist]`
Head, Tail	special notation
example	`[Head|Tail]`
Empty list	`[ ]`

SIMPLE EXTENSION OF MICRO-PROLOG

Chapter 2

Facts	argument predicate argument or predicate(arguments)

example	`Sally likes swimming or`
	`    likes(Sally swimming)`
	`Sally female or female(Sally)`

Constants	any word
example	Sally
Variables	one of the letters x, y or z, upper or lower case followed (optionally) by an integer
example	X1
Query	`is(Sally likes swimming)`
single answer	specify one
example	`one(x : x likes swimming)`
multiple answer	`all possibilities given`

example	`which(x : Sally likes x)`
	`swimming`
	`tennis`
	`no(more) answers`

Conjunctions	use the word AND or &
example	`which(x : x likes swimming  x`
	`likes tennis)`
Creating a database	access Prolog and LOAD SIMPLE prompt is &.
from user (to create	`add(<sentence>)`
interactively)	
example	`& .add((Sally likes swimming))`
from file (previously	`LOAD <file-name>`
created with editor or	
saved from past session)	
example	`LOAD STAR`
Options	accept, edit

Chapter 3

Rule	<simple sentence> if <sentence>
example	X exercises if X likes swimming
Rules with conjunction	use the word AND
example	X exercises if X likes swimming and X brought
	suit
Interrupt	^C CONTROL C

Chapter 4

| Trace | LOAD TRACE |
| | KILL TRACE |

Chapter 5

List	items in parentheses separated by spaces
example	(2 3 7)
Head, Tail	(t1 | t2)
example	(x | y)
Empty list	( )

C-PROLOG

Chapter 2

Facts	predicate(arguments).
example	`likes(sally,swimming).`
	`friendly(sally).`
	`shops(sally,vegetables,market).`

Constants	begin with a lower-case letter
example	sally
Variables	begin with an upper-case letter
example	Sport
Query	clause with or without variables follows a ?
example	`?- likes(sally,swimming).`
single answer	respond with a return

example	`?- likes(sally,Sport).`
	`Sport = swimming`
	`yes`

multiple answer	respond with a semi-colon

example	`?- likes(sally,Sport).`
	`Sport = swimming ,`
	`Sport = tennis ;`
	`no`

Conjunctions	use a comma for "and"
example	`?- likes(Who,swimming),` `    brought(Who,suit).`
Creating a database	access Prolog, get prompt |?-
from user (to inter- actively build database)	`consult(user).` or `[user].` `END_OF_INPUT (^D) to stop`

example	`| likes(sally,swimming).`
	`| ^D`
	`| ?-`

from file (previously built by editor or saved from past session)	`consult('<file-name>').` or `    ['<file-name>'].`
example	`['star.2'].` `STAR.2 CONSULTED`

Chapter 3

Rule	`<head> :- <body>.`
example	`gets_exercise(Who) :-` `    likes(Who,swimming)`
Rules with conjunction	use comma for conjunction

example	`gets_exercise(Who) :-`
	`    likes(Who,swimming),`
	`    brought(Who,suit).`

Interrupt	`^D CONTROL D`

Chapter 4

Trace	facility to observe processing
example	`?- trace.`
	`?- get_exercise(Who).`

Chapter 5

List	collection of objects specified in order
example	`[bank,store,florist]`
Head, Tail	special notation
example	`[Head|Tail].`
Empty list	`[ ]`
Notes:	C-Prolog allows real-number arithmetic

MICRO-PROLOG

Chapter 2

Facts	`((predicate argument1 argument2))`
example	`(likes Sally swimming)`
	`(female Sally)`
Constants	alpha character followed by letters or digits
example	Sally
Variables	one of the letters x, y or z, upper or lower case followed (optionally) by an integer
example	X1
Query	`? (likes Sally swimming)`
responses	? for no
	return to prompt for yes
show answer	specify to print variable instantiation
example	`((likes x swimming)(PP x))`
Conjunctions	sequence and enclose in parentheses
example	`((likes x swimming)(⌐ikes x tennis)(PP x))`
Creating a database	access Prolog
	prompt is &.
from user (to create interactively)	`((<sentence>))`
example	`& .((likes Sally swimming))`
from file (previously created with editor or saved from past session)	`LOAD <file-name>`
example	`LOAD STAR`

Chapter 3

Rule	`((<head>)(<body>))`
example	`((exercises X)(likes x swimming))`
Rules with conjunction	`((<head>)(<bodypt1>)(<bodypt2>)...)`
example	`((exercises X)(likes X`
	`swimming)(brought X suit))`
Interrupt	^C CONTROL C

Chapter 4

Trace	LOAD TRACE
	KILL TRACE

Chapter 5

List	items in parentheses separated by spaces
example	`(2 3 7)`
Head, Tail	`(t1 | t2)`
example	`(x | y)`
Empty list	`( )`

Appendix D

Formalizing Terminology

PROLOG COMPONENT SYNTAX

All components of a Turbo Prolog program are built from a few basic units. *Syntax* rules specify how these units can be combined to create other components. Turbo Prolog programs are made of terms. *Terms* can be *constants*, *variables* or *structures*. Constants and variables are simple entities; structures are collections of other entities that are aggregated into a single entity.

Constants are written as a sequence of characters. The characters are either alphanumeric (letters and numerals), in which case the sequence starts with a lower-case letter; non-alphanumeric printing characters (like '+'), called signs, in which case the constants are usually made entirely of signs; or all numerals, in which case they are treated as integers, or real numbers.

Variables are written as an alphanumeric sequence beginning with an upper case letter or with an underscore. In traces, Turbo Prolog represents variables as an underscore; the underscore, when used in clauses or goals, is the *anonymous variable*, a place-holder in a structure for a variable of no current relevance.

A structure, sometimes called a *compound term*, is made of a *functor* and *components*. The functor is written first and is followed by the components in parentheses. These components are terms: constants, variables or other structures. In Turbo Prolog, *predicates* and their *arguments* are expressed as structures. The predicate is a functor that is special because of its context, at the beginning of the structure. Functors that appear as components in a compound structure are treated as objects instead of as predicates, except in the case of certain built-in predicates such as not. The number of components with a functor is called the *arity* of the functor. Functors with two arguments are sometimes written as *operators* in *infix* form. These appear frequently in arithmetic expressions such as A + B.

Lists are an important type of structure in Turbo Prolog. They are made up of *elements* which are Turbo Prolog terms (i.e., constants, variables or structures). A list is either the empty list, noted as [ ], or is a structure with a *head* and *tail*.

By definition, the empty list is included as the last element of any list. A convenient notation, *list notation* is used to represent lists. Elements are enclosed in square brackets and separated by commas.

```
[X,Y,Z].
```

Special notation to separate the head and tail in list notation is the vertical bar.

```
[Head|Tail].
```

A list type must be declared by the programmer in the domains section. The standard data domains, which do not have to be declared, are *symbol, integer, real, file char* and *string*.

PROGRAM COMPONENTS

A Turbo Prolog program is made up of *sentences*. A sentence has a *head* and *body* which are separated by colon/hyphen (:-) and ends with a period. Either the head or the body may be empty. The head contains at most one term and the body may contain more. A sentence may be viewed *declaratively* so that

```
P :- Q,S.
```

means P is *true* if Q and S are true. A sentence may be viewed *procedurally* so that

```
P :- Q,S.
```

means P is a *goal* which succeeds if the subgoals, Q and S succeed.

If the head of the sentence is not empty, the sentence is called a *clause*. If the body of a clause is empty, it is called a *unit* clause and is written without the :-.

A sentence with an empty head is a *directive* specifically used for *questions* and is written as a goal.

There may be more than one clause with the same predicate for the head of the rule. Such multiple clauses allow alternatives for the rule. The group of one or more such clauses is called the *procedure* for that rule.

Turbo Prolog interpreters have some predicate definitions provided as part of the Turbo Prolog system. These definitions are known as *built-in predicates, built-in procedures* or *evaluable predicates*.

A significant number of the built-in predicates are *operators* used mainly for doing arithmetic in Turbo Prolog. Operators are assigned *precedence*, which is then used to determine which operation will be carried out first in the case of ambiguity.

TURBO PROLOG PROCESSING

In the *declarative semantics* of Turbo Prolog processing, the program attempts to prove the goal it has been given. The goal is or is not found *true*. A true *instance* of a goal is found by the success of the same goal in the head of a clause in the program. That clause's subgoals must succeed with any variables having been instantiated to the same constants as those in the goal.

Declaratively, Turbo Prolog processing *activates* the goal. Procedurally, Turbo Prolog processing *calls* the procedure or *executes* the goal.

The system starts at the top of the program and searches for a clause whose head *matches* or *unifies* with the goal so it can satisfy the goal. If a match is found, any goals in the body of the clause are executed in a manner like the first. Throughout the process, unification results in *instantiation* of variables. If some subgoal fails, *backtracking* begins and variables are uninstantiated (in the reverse order), as necessary, so that attempts to resatisfy a goal or subgoal can be made.

FOUNDATION IN LOGIC

Turbo Prolog is based on a formal logic system called *predicate calculus*. The form of clauses in Turbo Prolog is that of *Horn clauses*, in that, at most, one atomic expression appears to the left of the :- sign. Turbo Prolog's processing uses *resolution* to carry out its tasks and follows a *depth-first* rather than *breadth-first* search strategy.

For further discussion of the formalisms and foundation of Turbo Prolog, see the articles and books listed in Appendix B, Further Reading.

Answers to Exercises

CHAPTER 1

1.1.1   `ate <food> <meal>`

1.1.2   `ate <food> <meal> <day>`

1.1.3   `ate <food> <day> <meal>`
       `ate <day> <food> <meal>`
       `ate <day> <meal> <food>`

1.1.4   `july 1,2 school`
       `july  3   rest`
       `july  4   travel`
       `july <weeks> <do>`

1.2.1

1.2.2 Note these are ambiguous. One might be "Joe gave the borrowed money to Sarah, who had owed some to Jane." "Joe borrowed money from Sarah; Jane had owed Sarah money too." My office is lighted by a window, cooled by an air conditioner and painted beige, which is a kind of brown. In it I have a desk. I have the key that gives access to it.

1.3.1 Many choices `<object>` `<does something>`
                    `<object>` `<is something>`

1.3.2 Cool: sandals, shorts
Warm: sweaters, long sox
Nice gifts: flowers, sweaters

1.3.3 Not cool: sweaters, long sox, flowers
Not warm: sandals, shorts, flowers
Not nice gifts: sandals, shorts, long sox

1.4.1

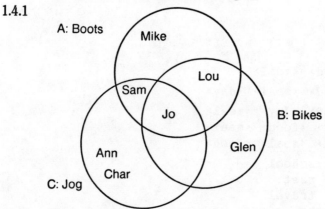

1.4.2 Jo, Lou

1.4.3 Jo

1.4.4 Mike, Sam, Jo, Lou, Glen

1.4.5 Everybody

CHAPTER 2

2.1.1 ```
on(book,table).
on(book,third_shelf).
owns(john,dog).
owns(jim,cat).
```

2.1.2  Sarah is Jane's mother.
Sarah's mother is Jane.
Joe is father to Sam.
Sam is father to Joe.
```

2.1.3   In this joke the word "nothing" means two different things in its two uses. Turbo Prolog would assume it means the same thing at all times.

2.2.1   (database as above)
```
Goal: on(book,Where).
Goal: on(What,third_shelf).
Goal: owns(john,What).
Goal: owns(jim,Animal).
```

2.2.2
```
Thief = john
A = dog
Breed = jersey
```

2.2.3   Breed is a meaningful name, but A is not. Thief is meaningful but may not convey the meaning intended.

2.3.1
```
What = call_agent
What = write_home
2 solutions
What = get_money
What = study
2 solutions
When = thursday
When = tuesday
2 solutions
```

2.3.2   seven

2.4.1   `Day = friday  Task = get_tickets`

2.4.2   `Goal: do(__,study).`

2.4.3   `Goal: do(When,What),do(When,study).`

CHAPTER 3

3.1.1   `false`

3.1.2   `wear(shorts) :- high(seventies).`

3.1.3   `plan(picnic) :- rain(none).`

3.2.1
```
Day = sunday
Day = tuesday
Day = wednesday
3 solutions
```

3.2.2   `take(umbrella,Day) :- weather(Day,rainy).`

3.2.3   `take(umbrella,Day) :- weather(Day,overcast).`

3.3.1
```
mixed_feelings(birders,Day) :-
               weather(Day,rainy),
               active(birds,Day).
```

3.3.2   it won't

3.4.1
```
Whom = bet
Whom = cat
2 solutions
Whom = bet
Whom = cat
2 solutions
Who = ann
Who = abe
2 solutions
```

3.4.2
```
Goal: married(Her,Him).
Goal: mother(__,Person),father(__,Person).
```

3.5.1
```
Older = ann,   Younger = bet
Older = ann,   Younger = cat
Older = bet,   Younger = may
Older = may,   Younger = nan
Older = abe,   Younger = bet
Older = abe,   Younger = cat
Older = ann,   Younger = may
Older = ann,   Younger = nan
Older = bet,   Younger = nan
Older = abe,   Younger = may
Older = abe,   Younger = nan
11 solutions
```

3.5.2
```
glump(joe,sally).
glump(sam,joe).
glump(may,joe).
glump(leo,may).
glump(sister,leo).
knows(sally).
knows(Person) :- glump(Person,Teacher),
                 knows(Teacher).
```

3.6.1   The same two answers will be reported over and over, then the system will run out of internal space. An oscillating recursion is set up with mother and father.
One or the other of these rules should not be included.

3.6.2   The "do" predicate may keep reusing itself without finding a stopping condition.

CHAPTER 4

4.1.1   Seven

4.1.2   Turbo Prolog will not be aware of any problem or contradiction.

4.2.1 Four values if we still have the duplicate for friday.

4.2.2
```
Outlook = rainy
Outlook = fair
2 solutions
```

4.3.1
```
Footgear = shoes,   Hue = black
Footgear = shoes,   Hue = white
Footgear = sneakers,  Hue = red
Footgear = skates,  Hue = white
Footgear = running_shoes,  Hue = black
5 solutions
```

4.3.2 All the earlier responses would be given, plus a set that report Foot gear = sox for each color of sox, too. Because Turbo Prolog is simply matching on the pattern, sox are the same as footgear in the same predicate and a duplicated match can be found by searching for the same predicate twice (9 solutions).

4.4.1
```
happy(birders,When)                    found rule line 14
   weather(When,fair)                  instantiate When
   weather(sunday,fair)                found fact line 1
      active(birds,sunday)             found fact line 16
When = sunday                          reported
   weather(When,fair)                  instantiate When
      weather(tuesday,fair)            found fact line 3
      active(birds,tuesday)            found fact line 17
When = tuesday                         reported
   weather(When,fair)                  instantiate When
   weather(wednesday,fair)             found fact line 4
      active(birds,wednesday)          no match
   weather(When,fair)                  no match
   observed(rarebird,When)             instantiate When
   observed(rarebird,wednesday)        found fact line ,7
When = wednesday                       reported
   observed(rarebird,When)             instantiate When
   observed(rarebird,tuesday)          found fact line 20
When = tuesday                         reported
4 solutions
```

4.4.2 The first match attempted would be to eyes(Hue,Person) which wouiu instantiate the variable Person to sue, then sky color would be sought for the next match (3 solutions). After all these, other matches for the first part would be sought (there are none).

4.5.1
```
ancestor(Older,Younger).
parent(Older,Younger).
mother(Older,Younger).
mother(ann,Younger).
mother(ann,bet).
Older = ann,   Younger = bet
```

4.5.2
```
Older = ann,  Younger = bet
Older = bet,  Younger = may
Older = ann,  Younger = cat
Older = may,  Younger = nan
Older = abe,  Younger = bet
Older = abe,  Younger = cat
Older = ann,  Younger = may
Older = ann,  Younger = nan
Older = bet,  Younger = nan
Older = abe,  Younger = may
Older = abe,  Younger = nan
11 solutions
```

CHAPTER 5

5.1.1 `[red,orange,yellow,green,blue,indigo,violet]`

5.1.2
```
rainbow([red,orange,yellow,green,blue,
                            indigo,violet]).
```

5.1.3
```
Goal:rainbow(__,__,__,__,__,__,violet]).
Goal:rainbow(__,__,__,__,__,__,purple]).
```

5.2.1
```
Head = red  Tail = [orange,yellow]
Head = red  Tail = [orange]
Head = red  Tail = []
none; the empty list has no head nor tail
```

5.2.2
```
Head = k_wilhelm  Tail = [juniper_time,fault_
lines]
Head = u_leguin   Tail = [left_hand_of_darkness]
2 solutions
```

5.2.3 `Goal: author([Name__]).`

5.3.1
```
List = [k_wilhelm,juniper_time,fault_lines]
Element = k_wilhelm
List = [k_wilhelm,juniper_time,fault_lines]
Element = juniper_time
List = [k_wilhelm,juniper_time,fault_lines]
Element = fault_lines
List = [u_leguin,left_hand_of_darkness]
Element = u_leguin
List = [u_leguin,left_hand_of_darkness]
Element = left_hand_of_darkness
List = [l_m_alcott,little_women]
Element = l_m_alcott
```

```
          List · [l_m_alcott,little_women]
          Element = little_women
          7 solutions
```

5.3.2　Goal: author(What).

5.4.1
```
          List = [k_wilhelm,juniper_time,fault_lines]
          List = [u_leguin,left_hand_of_darkness]
          List = [l_m_alcott,little_women]
```

5.4.2
```
          clean_cut(Dwarf) :- dwarves(List1),
                             no_beard(List2),
                             member(Dwarf,List1),
                             member(Dwarf,List2).
```

5.4.3
```
          What = condor
          What = cardinal
          What = crane
          What = bluebird
          What = sparrow
          (user interrupt)
```

5.5.1　Use third_place, as it implies at least two books.

5.5.2
```
          author_names(Which) :- author(List),
                                front(Which,List).
```

5.5.3
```
          Goal: rainbow(List),last(violet,List).
          Goal: rainbow(List),last(purple,List).
```

5.6.1
```
          List = [condor,crane,sparrow]
          Result = [frigate_bird,condor,crane,sparrow]
          List = [bluebird,cardinal]
          Result = [frigate_bird,bluebird,cardinal]
          2 solutions
          List = [bluebird,cardinal]   What = [bluebird]
          1 solution
          List = [condor,crane,sparrow]
          Result =
                 [condor,crane,sparrow,condor,crane,sparrow]
          List = [bluebird,cardinal]
          Result = [bluebird,cardinal,bluebird,cardinal]
          2 solutions
          L1 = [condor,crane,sparrow]
          L2 = [condor,crane,sparrow]
          Result =
                 [condor,crane,sparrow,condor,crane,sparrow]
          L1 = [condor,crane,sparrow]
          L2 = [bluebird,cardinal]
          Result = [condor,crane,sparrow,bluebird,cardinal]
```

```
        L1 = [bluebird,cardinal]
        L2 = [condor,crane,sparrow]
        Result =
                  [bluebird,cardinal,condor,crane,sparrow]
        L1 = [bluebird,cardinal]
        L2 = [bluebird,cardinal]
        Result = [bluebird,cardinal,bluebird,cardinal]
        4 solutions
```

5.6.2
```
        List = [condor,crane,sparrow]
        Result = [sparrow,crane,condor]
        List = [bluebird,cardinal]
        Result = [cardinal,bluebird]
        2 solutions
        List = [condor,crane,sparrow]
        Result = [condor,crane,sparrow,
                              sparrow,crane,condor]
        List = [bluebird,cardinal]
        Result = [bluebird,cardinal,cardinal,bluebird]
        2 solutions
        no solution (none of the rarebird lists is a
        palindrome)
```

5.6.3
```
        odd_pal(Half,Result) :- append(Half,Tail,Result),
                                reverse(Half,[H|Tail]).
```

5.7.1
```
        a) legal
        b) legal
        c) legal
        d) not legal
        e) not legal
```

5.7.2
```
        What = [l[a,b,c],s(dog),s(cat)]
        What = s(dog)
        What = cat
```

CHAPTER 6

6.1.1   Descriptively: your paragraph should use the terms "defined" and "is related to" or such expressions that concern the meaning of the rules. Prescriptively: your paragraph should use terms like "process," talk about the order things happen, or express the idea of change over time.

6.1.2

6.2.1
```
ancestor(Old,Young) :- parent(Old,Young).
ancestor(Old,Young) :-
        ancestor(Old,Mid),parent(Mid,Young).
ancestor(Old,Young) :- parent(Old,Young).
ancestor(Old,Young) :-
        parent(Mid,Young),ancestor(Old,Mid).
```
The second is preferable because it controls the recursion.

6.2.2
```
parent(joe,sam).
parent(sam,jay).
parent(jay,rod).
parent(rod,lou).
ancestor(Old,Young) :- parent(Old,Young).
ancestor(Old,Young) :-
        parent(Mid,Young),ancestor(Old,Mid).
descendant(Y,O) :- parent(O,Y).
descendant(Y,O) :-
        descendant(Y,M),parent(O,M).
(or descendant(Y,O) :- ancestor(O,Y).)
```

6.3.1
```
When = tuesday
1 solution
```

6.3.2
```
When = tuesday
1 solution
```

6.3.3 `holiday(friday,july_4).`

6.4.1
```
order(Vegetable) :- green(Vegetable),!,fail.
order(Vegetable).
```

6.4.2
```
a) order(Vegetable) :- not(green(Vegetable)),
                         not(yellow(Vegetable)).
b) order(Vegetable) :- not(green(Vegetable)).
   order(Vegetable) :- not(yellow(Vegetable)).
```
c) The vegetable must be both green and yellow.

CHAPTER 7

7.1.1 Input and output are dependent on sequence of processing. Since sequence is critical, so is time and work over time is more of a procedural concept than a definitional concept.

7.1.2 cut; fail; exit; recursion; a rule that always succeeds like "repeat"; internal vs. external goals

7.2.1 a) The first part of the magic rule selects out words of 4 characters.

b) `magic(Old,New) :- frontchar(Old,'a',_),`
`                          upper_lower(New,Old).`

c) `magic(is,"IS").`
`   magic(did,"DID").`

7.2.2 Leading zeros would be suppressed in the numbers.

7.3.1 `forecast(Plan) :- findall(D,weather(D,_),Plan).`

7.3.2 `similar(Days) :- weather(_,Outlook),`
`                      findall(D,weather(D,Outlook),Days).`

7.3.3 `ex(Object) :- retract(idea(Object)),`
`                  concat("x",Object,Answer),`
`                  asserta(idea(Answer)).`

CHAPTER 8

8.1.1 Several, because only_one is open and so is the screen, plus the other predefined devices, the printer and communication port. The predefined devices are always open.

8.1.2 a) Put the values (or variables) in the single write statement before the "\n" string.

b) Put a "\n" string between each of the values in the write statement.

8.2.1
```
predicates
   choose_response(symbol,string)
clauses
   choose_response(october,
                    "That's this month!") :- !.
   choose_response(_,"That's a while yet.").
goal
   write("What month is your birthday?   "),
   readln(Month),
   choose_response(Month,Answer),
   write("\n",Answer).
```

8.2.2
```
goal
  makewindow(1,25,32,"one",0,0,25,80),
  cursor(1,39),
  write("This is 1"),
  readchar(_),
  makewindow(2,42,32,"two",10,20,10,20),
  cursor(1,9),
  write("This is 2"),
  readchar(_),
  shiftwindow(1),
  cursor(2,39),
  write("This is 1 again. Press space bar.").
```

8.3.1
```
trace
domains
  file = only_one
goal
  trace(off),
  write("Type an integer  "),
  readint(Value),
  openwrite(only_one,"one.dat"),
  writedevice(only_one),
  write(Value,"\n"),
  closefile(only_one),
  openread(only_one,"one.dat"),
  readdevice(only_one),
  trace(on),
  readint(Again),
  writedevice(screen),
  write(Again),
  closefile(only_one).
```

8.3.2
```
predicates
  repeat
clauses
  repeat.
  repeat :- repeat.
goal
  repeat, readchar(Key),
          Key = 'e',
  edit("this string",Return).
```

CHAPTER 9

9.1.1   20
         26
         14

9.1.2   ```
do(X,Y,Z) :-
        X = (2) + (3 * 4 + 6),
        Y = (2 + 3) * 4 + 6,
        Z = (2 + 3 * 4) + 6 mod 2.
```

9.2.1   ```
facts of the form temp(high,<value>).
ave_high(Val) :-
    findall(Each,temp(high,Each),Bg),
    length(Bg,Num), sum(Bg,Sm), Val = Sm / Num.
```

9.2.2   ```
double(Old,Young) :- person(Old,O_age),
                     person(Young,Y_age),
                     O_age = (Y_age * 2).
```

9.2.3   ```
age_plus_ten(Subject) :- person(Subject,Age),!,
                         person(Other,Other_age),
                         Other_age > Age+10,
                         write(Other), fail.
```

9.3.1   Switch the >= sign for <=

9.3.2   Duplicate values would be placed before the existing value instead of jafter it. The result would be the same.

9.3.3   It will work as written except in the domains declaration and the insert predicate, change integer to symbol.

CHAPTER 10

10.1.1

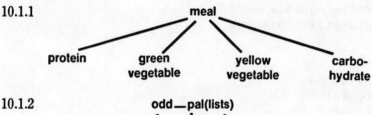

10.1.2

10.1.3   ```
valid_paln(L) :- palindrome(Half,L).
valid_paln(L) :- odd_pal(Part,L).
```
```

10.2.1 The rule first goes into the recursion and then out; value in shown in left column, out in right.

```
T = [6,3]   S = 3
S = ?       R = 2
T = [3]     S = 2
S = ?       R = 1
T = []      S = 1
S = 0       R = 0
```

10.2.2
```
Goal: reverse([a,b],R).
Goal: append([a,b],[x,y],R).
Goal: palindrome([ ],R).
```

10.3.1 These are the previous rules for reverse, append and palindrome. The components of the mutiple rules must be grouped together. Names that are more communicative should be used.

10.3.2
```
have_groceries :- stock(starch),
        stock(protein),stock(sweets).
stock(starch) :- cereal(Brand),
                     supper_dish(Pasta).
stock(protein) :- sandwich(Filling),milk(white).
stock(sweets) :- juice(Fruit),pie(Type).
```

10.3.3
```
stock(sweets) :- juice(Fruit),pie(Type),
                    (Fruit <> Type).
```

General Index

Throughout the General Index, bold face indicates built-in predicates. An Index to Built-in Predicates follows (see page 213) along with a separate Index to Examples on page 215.

Index to Built-In Predicates

Index to Examples